CHRIST SET FORTH

CHRIST SET FORTH

In His Death, Resurrection, Ascension,
Sitting at God's Right Hand, and Intercession
As the *Cause* of Justification, and
The *Object* of Justifying Faith,
from Romans 8:34.

Thomas Goodwin

Who is he that condemneth? It is Christ that died, yea rather,
that is risen again, who is even at the right hand of God,
who also maketh intercession for us.
ROMANS 8:34.

THE BANNER OF TRUTH TRUST

THE BANNER OF TRUTH TRUST
3 Murrayfield Road, Edinburgh EH12 6EL, UK
P.O. Box 621, Carlisle, PA 17013, USA

*

First published in 1642
Reprinted from the 1862 Nichol edition of
The Works of Thomas Goodwin, vol. 4
This edition © The Banner of Truth Trust, 2015

ISBNs
Print: 978-1-84871-558-5
EPUB: 978-1-84871-560-8
Kindle: 978-1-84871-561-5

*

Typeset in 11/15 pt Sabon Oldstyle Figures at
The Banner of Truth Trust, Edinburgh.

Printed in the USA by
Versa Press, Inc.,
East Peoria, IL

Editorial Note:

Footnotes from the Nichol edition of Goodwin's *Works* are attributed to 'Ed.' The present publisher has included a few additional footnotes—these are attributed to 'P.' Some spellings have been modernised. Greek words have been transliterated, and along with many Latin phrases are explained in the footnotes where necessary.

Contents

Section 1

———

Showing by way of introduction that Christ is the example and object of justifying faith.

Section 2

————

Christ the object and support of faith for justification, in his death.

1. How not Christ's person simply, but Christ as dying, is the object of faith as justifying, p. 29.

2. What in Christ's death, faith seeking justification, is especially to eye and look at, p. 35.

3. What support or matter of triumph Christ's death affords to faith for justification, p. 43.

Section 3

————

Faith supported by Christ's resurrection.

1. Christ's resurrection supporteth faith two ways: 1. By being an evidence of our justification; 2. By having an influence into our justification.—The necessity of Christ's resurrection, for the procuring our justification, p. 55.

2. For the explanation of both these is shown, how Christ sustained a double relation first, of a surety given for us; secondly, of a common person in our stead. The difference of these two, and the usefulness of these two

Section 4

——

Faith supported by Christ's ascension, and sitting at God's right hand.

Section 5

The triumph of faith from Christ's intercession.

Foreword

It is hoped that this new typeset edition of one of Thomas Goodwin's most beloved and enduring works will bless a new generation of readers. It is a book full of theological riches and penetrating pastoral insights.

It should be pointed out that this book is not an abridgement of the original. It is rather a faithful reproduction of the version found in volume 4 of the *Works of Thomas Goodwin*, which was published as part of the Nichol series of Puritan reprints in 1862. In this Banner of Truth Puritan Paperbacks edition it appears in a much more attractive typesetting which makes Goodwin's valuable little work more accessible to modern readers.

Thomas Goodwin was born in 1600 in Rollesby, a village near Norwich in the south-east of England. During his nearly eighty years he became an important and influential figure in the religious and political issues of his day. He was educated at Cambridge where he came under the influence of John Preston and Richard Sibbes. Goodwin became a well-loved lecturer, preacher, and pastor. He rose in prominence in the Puritan movement, and was subsequently a frequent preacher before Parliament, a prominent member of the Westminster Assembly, a personal chaplain to Oliver Cromwell, and the President of Magdalen College, Oxford. When England restored the monarchy in 1660, and the Puritans found themselves out of favour, Goodwin continued to preach and write until his death in 1680. Most of his books published during his lifetime (including *Christ Set Forth*), appeared in their first editions between the years 1636 to the mid 1640s. After his death, his son edited and printed five extensive volumes of unpublished manuscripts which Goodwin had amassed during his prodigious lifetime. His legacy and writings have been a blessing to countless Christians.

Though rich in theology and pastoral insight, *Christ Set Forth* is primarily a book written to encourage Christians. It is a guidebook for keeping one's heart and faith pointed in the right direction, towards Christ himself. In it Goodwin pushes aside anything that might displace Christ in one's heart. In chapter after chapter he sets forth the glory of Christ and his work as mediator as the only object of one's faith and affection.

Goodwin wrote this book out of deep personal and pastoral concern. He explains in his introduction that he had seen many believers stray in their faith by looking into their own hearts for signs of grace instead of looking away from themselves to Christ. This tendency arose out of the quest for the assurance of salvation, a hot topic in Goodwin's day. Much time and effort was spent in examining one's life and soul to detect signs and evidences of saving grace. While biblically motivated this search for internal signs can easily divert the attention of the believer from Christ. How subtle the temptation for the soul to cling to these internal evidences and treat them as the sole ground of confidence before God. On the other hand, many a believer looks within and sees little to inspire confidence and bring a sense of assurance. In both cases, Christ, who is the believer's only true confidence and hope, is no longer the focus.

We know that this was a problem for Goodwin in early life. In the biography compiled by his son he says

> I was diverted from Christ for several years, to search only into the signs of grace in me: it was almost seven years e'er I was taken off to live by faith on Christ, and God's free love, which are alike the object of Faith.

The search for signs of saving grace within somewhat unhinged Goodwin, even to the extent of his neglecting Christ as the sole object of his faith. When he writes in the introduction to this work of those 'many holy and precious souls' who have become carried away from Christ, he is speaking out of his own personal experience.

The remedy for this misplaced focus is a rich and full exposition of Christ's saving work, and that is

Goodwin's object in writing this book. In it the author sets forth the finished, yet continuing, work of Christ as the only object of a believer's faith. Goodwin glories in Christ the Mediator and teaches believers to rest in the Saviour's redeeming work. 'Who will condemn?' since Christ has done all to secure the salvation of the elect.

May this book be an encouragement to your faith. You may not face precisely the same struggles Goodwin faced and many of his fellow Christians faced in the seventeenth century. Nevertheless, with Goodwin you may learn to revel in the saving work of Christ for sinners and admire the way in which he has accomplished it. Take joy in the Bible's promises that point to Christ as the one who justifies completely. Be blessed by Goodwin's warm, pastoral exhortations as he points you in the right direction. And having read this book, may you walk with confidence in the light of that glorious scriptural declaration: 'Who is he that condemns? It is Christ that died, yea rather, that is risen again, who is even at the right hand of God, who also makes intercession for us.' You will find no greater foundation on which to rest your confidence.

Scott T. Berggren
Bandung, Indonesia
December 2014

Author's Introduction

To the Reader,

What the scope of this treatise itself is, the title-page and the table of contents will sufficiently inform you: I shall only here acquaint you with what was mine, in a few words. I have by long experience observed many holy and precious souls, who have clearly and wholly given up themselves to Christ, to be saved by him his own way, and who at their first conversion (as also at times of desertion) have made an entire and immediate close with Christ alone for their justification, who yet in the ordinary course and way of their spirits have been too much carried away with the rudiments of Christ in their own hearts, and not after Christ himself: the stream of their more constant thoughts and deepest intentions running in the channel of reflecting upon, and searching into the gracious dispositions of their own hearts, so to bring down, or to raise up (as the apostle's words are, Rom. 10:8), and so get a sight of Christ by them. Whereas Christ himself is 'nigh them' (as the apostle there speaks), if they would but nakedly look upon himself through thoughts of pure and single faith.

Although the use of our own graces, by way of sign and evidence of Christ in us, be allowed us by God, and is no way derogatory from Christ, if subordinated to faith; and so as the heart be not too inordinate and immoderate in poring too long or too much on them, to fetch their comfort from them, unto a neglect of Christ: yet as pleasures that are lawful are unlawfully used when our thoughts and intentions are too long, or too frequent, or too vehement in them, so as to dead the heart, either to the present delighting in God, or pursuing after him, with the joint strength of our souls, as our only chiefest good: so an immoderate recourse unto signs (though barely considered as such), is as unwarrantable, when thereby we are diverted and taken off from a more constant actual exercise of daily thoughts of faith towards Christ immediately, as he is set forth to be our righteousness, either by the way of assurance (which is a kind of enjoyment of him), or recumbency and renewed adherence in pursuit after him.

And yet the minds of many are so wholly taken up with their own hearts, that (as the Psalmist says of God) Christ 'is scarce in all their thoughts'. But let these consider what a dishonour this must needs be unto Christ, that his train and favourites (our graces) should have a fuller court and more frequent attendance from our hearts than himself, who is the 'King of Glory'. And likewise what a shame also it is for believers themselves, who are his spouse, to look upon their husband no otherwise but by reflection and at second hand, through the intervention and assistance of their own graces, as mediators between him and them.

Now to rectify this error, the way is not wholly to reject all use of such evidences, but to order them, both for the season, as also the issue of them. For the season, so as that the use of them go not before, but still should follow after an address of faith first renewed, and acts thereof put forth upon Christ himself. Thus whensoever we would go down into our own hearts, and take a view of our graces, let us be sure first to look wholly out of ourselves unto Christ, as our justification, and to close with him immediately; and this as if we had no present or by-past grace to evidence our being in him. And if then, whilst faith is thus immediately clasping about Christ, as sitting upon his throne of grace, we find either present or fore-past graces coming in as handmaids, to attend and witness to the truth of this adherence unto Christ (as after such single and absolute acts of faith it oftentimes falls out);—the Holy Ghost (without whose light they shine not) 'bearing witness *with* our spirits', that is, our graces, as well as *to* our spirits;—and then again, for the issue of them, if in the closure of all, we again let fall our viewing and comforting ourselves in them, or this their testimony, and begin afresh (upon his encouragement) to act faith upon Christ immediately with a redoubled strength; if thus (I say) we make such evidences to be subservient only unto faith (whilst it makes Christ its Alpha and Omega, the beginning and the end of all), this will be no prejudice at all to Christ's glory, or the workings of faith itself; for by this course the life of faith is still actually maintained and kept upon wing in its full use and exercise towards Christ alone for justification. Whereas many Christians do habitually make that only but as a supposed or taken for granted principle, which they seldom use, but have laid up for a time of need; but actually live more in the view and comfort of their own graces, and the gracious workings thereof in the duties towards Christ.

The reason of this defect, among many others, I have attributed partly to a 'barrenness' (as Peter's phrase is) 'in the knowledge of the Lord Jesus Christ', and of such things revealed about him, as might be matter for faith to work and feed upon: as also to a want of skill (whilst men want assurance) to bend and bow, and subjugate to the use of a faith for mere adherence, all those things that they know and hear of Christ as made justification unto us. It being in experience a matter of the greatest difficulty (and yet certainly most feasible and attainable), for such a faith as can yet only rely and cast itself upon Christ for justification, yet rightly to take in, and so to make use of all that which is or may be said of Christ, his being made righteousness to us, in his death, resurrection, *etc.*, as to quicken and strengthen itself in such acts of mere adherence, until assurance itself comes, for whose use and entertainment all truths lie more fair and directly to be received by it. They all serve as a fore-right wind to assurance of faith, to fill the sails thereof, and carry on with a more full and constant gale (as the word used by the apostle for assurance[1] imports), whereas to the faith of a poor recumbent, they serve but as a half side-wind, unto which yet, through skill, the sails of such a faith may be so turned and applied towards it, as to carry a soul on with much ease and quietness unto Christ the desired haven; it notwithstanding waiting all that while for a more fair and full gale of assurance in the end.

Now to help or instruct believers in that latter, namely, the use of such a skill, is not directly the drift of this treatise, I having reserved that part (if God assist me and give leisure, and this find acceptance) unto another about the *Acts of Justifying Faith*, wherein this art now mentioned is to be the main scope.[2] That which I have here endeavoured, is, to set forth to all sorts of believers (whether they have assurance or not) Christ as he is the object of our faith as justifying, and as the cause of justification to us; and so I send forth this as a premise and preparatory to that other. And to that purpose I

---

[1] Viz. πληροφορία [*plerophoria*].—Ed.

[2] *Of the Object and Acts of Justifying Faith, Works of Thomas Goodwin*, vol. 4 (1697); repr. as vol. 8 of the Nichol edition (1864); repr. by the Banner of Truth Trust (1985).—P.

have run over some few articles of our faith or creed, as I found them put together in one bundle by the great apostle, namely Christ, in his death, resurrection, ascension, sitting at God's right hand, and intercession, and have handled these no further than as in all these he is made Justification unto us, therein having punctually kept unto the apostle's scope. By all which you may (in the mean time) see, what abundant provision God hath laid up in Christ (in the point of justification) for all sorts of believers to live upon: every thing in Christ, whatsoever he was, or whatsoever he did, with a joint voice speaking justification unto us. You may see also that God hath in Christ justified us over and over; and thereby come to discern what little reason you have to suffer your hearts to be carried aside to other comforters, and so be spoiled and bereft of these more immediately prepared, and laid up for us in Christ himself. To have handled all those considerations, which his obedience unto death affords unto the justification of a believer, and his comfort therein, in this small tractate, would have made that part too disproportioned to the rest: it alone deserves, and will require a distinct tract, which therefore I have cast into another method;[1] and so in this treatise have touched only upon what may for the present be sufficient to furnish that part, to keep company with its fellows. Only when I had thus presented Christ along

[1] See footnote on p. 45.—P.

from his death, resurrection, and ascension, unto his sitting in heaven, and there performing that great part of his priesthood, the work of intercession, I judged it both homogeneal to all these, and conducing to the greater encouragement of believers in the exercise of their faith, to subjoin that to the other treatise, How Christ's Heart, now he is in Heaven, stands affected to us sinners here below.[1] And a better token (take the argument itself, if I could have fuller represented it) how to present unto his spouse I know not, than a true character of her Husband's heart, now he is in glory: and (but for method's sake) I would have placed it first, it being more suited to vulgar capacities, whose benefit I aim at. Now in that discourse I confess I have not aimed to keep so strictly unto the matter of justification only, as in the other I have done; but have more generally discussed it, and shown how his heart stands towards us, under all sorts of infirmities whatsoever, either of sin or misery, yet so as it will serve for the matter of justification also. The Father of our Lord Jesus Christ grant us according to the riches of his glory, that Christ may dwell in our hearts by faith, and that we may know the love of Christ, which passeth knowledge! Amen.

---

[1] *The Heart of Christ in Heaven, Towards Sinners on Earth* (1642), repr. in vol. 4 of the Nichol edition (1862). Also available as *The Heart of Christ* in the Puritan Paperback series (Edinburgh: Banner of Truth Trust, 2011). As Goodwin indicates, the above treatise was published together with his *Christ Set Forth*—P.

SECTION 1

SHOWING BY WAY OF INTRODUCTION THAT CHRIST IS THE EXAMPLE AND OBJECT OF JUSTIFYING FAITH

Who is he that condemneth? It is Christ that died, yea rather, that is risen again, who is even at the right hand of God, who also maketh intercession for us.

ROM. 8:34.

Chapter 1

The scope of these words: that they were Christ's originally.—Christ the highest example of believing.—Encouragements to our faith from thence.

These words are a triumphing challenge uttered by the apostle in the name of all the *elect*; for so he begins it in verse 33 foregoing, 'Who shall lay anything to the charge of God's *elect*? It is God that justifies.' And then follow these words, 'Who shall condemn?' namely, God's elect. 'It is Christ that died,' *etc*. This challenge we find first published by Jesus Christ himself, our only champion, Isa. 50 (a chapter made of and for Christ), verse 8, 'He is near that justifies me; who will contend with me?' They were Christ's words there, and spoken of God's justifying him: and these are every believer's words here, intended of God's justifying them. Christ is brought in there uttering them as standing at the high priest's tribunal, when they spat upon him, and buffeted him, as verses 4, 5; when he was condemned by Pilate, then he exercised

3

this faith on God his Father, 'He is near that justifies me.' And as in that his condemnation he stood in our stead, so in this his hope of his justification he speaks in our stead also, and as representing us in both. And upon this the apostle here pronounces, in like words, of all the elect, 'It is God that justifies; who shall accuse?' Christ was condemned, yea, 'hath died; who therefore shall condemn?' Lo, here the communion we have with Christ in his death and condemnation, yea in his very faith; if he trusted in God, so may we, and shall as certainly be delivered. Observe we first from hence, by way of premise to all that follows,

Observe: That Christ lived by faith as well as we do.

In John 1:16, we are said to 'receive of his fullness grace for grace'; that is, grace answerable and like unto his; and so (among others) faith.

For explication hereof.

First; in some sense he had a faith for justification like unto ours, though not a justification through faith, as we have. He went not, indeed, out of himself, to rely on another for righteousness, for he had enough of his own (he being 'the Lord our righteousness'); yet he believes on God to justify him, and had recourse to God for justification: 'He is near', says he, 'that justifies me.' If he had stood in his own person merely, and upon his own bottom[1] only, there had been no occasion for such a speech; and yet consider him as he stood in our stead, there was; for what need of such a justification, if he had not been some way near a condemnation? He therefore must be supposed to stand here (in Isaiah) at God's tribunal, as well as at Pilate's, with all our sins upon him. And so the same prophet tells us, chap. 53:6, 'God made the iniquities of us to meet on him.' He was now made sin, and a curse, and stood not in danger of Pilate's condemnation only, but of God's too, unless he satisfied him for all those sins. And when the wrath of God for sin came thus in upon him, his faith was put to it, to trust and wait on him for his justification, for to take off all those sins, together with his wrath from off him, and to acknowledge himself satisfied and him acquitted. Therefore, in Psalm 22 (which was made for Christ when hanging on the cross, and speaks how his heart was taken up that while), he is brought in as putting forth such a faith as here we speak of, when he called God his God, 'My God! my God!' then, when as to his sense, he had forsaken him, 'Why hast thou forsaken me?' Yea, he helped his faith with the faith of the forefathers, whom upon their trust in him God had delivered; 'Our fathers',

---

[1] basis; foundation. — P.

saith he, 'trusted in thee; they trusted, and thou didst deliver them.' Yea, at verse 5, we find him laying himself at God's feet, lower than ever any man did. 'I am a worm', says he (which every man treads on, and counts it a matter of nothing for to kill), 'and no man', as it follows; and all this, because he bare our sins. Now his deliverance and justification from all these, to be given him at his resurrection, was the matter, the business he thus trusted in God for, even that he should rise again, and be acquitted from them. So Psa. 16 (a psalm made also for Christ, when to suffer, and lie in the grave), verses 8-10: 'The Lord is at my right hand, I shall not be moved: Therefore my heart is glad, my flesh also resteth in hope', or, as in the original, 'dwells in confident sureness'. 'Thou wilt not leave my soul in hell', that is, under the load of these sins, and thy wrath laid on me for them; 'neither wilt suffer thy Holy One [in my body] to see corruption.' This is in substance all one with what is here said in this one word, 'He is near that justifies me', for Christ's resurrection was a justification of him, as I shall hereafter show.

Neither, 2, did he exercise faith for himself only, but for us also, and that more than any of us is put to it, to exercise for himself; for he in dying, and emptying himself, trusted God with the merit of all his sufferings aforehand, there being many thousands of souls to be saved thereby a long while after, even to the end of the world. He died and betrusted all that stock into his Father's hands, to give it out in grace and glory, as those for whom he died should have need. And this is a greater trust (considering the infinite number of his elect as then yet to come) than any man hath occasion to put forth for himself alone. God trusted Christ before he came into the world, and saved many millions of the Jews upon his bare word. And then Christ, at his death, trusts God again as much, both for the salvation of Jews and Gentiles, that were to believe after his death. In Heb. 2:12-15, it is made an argument that Christ was a man like us, because he was put to live by faith like as we are (which the angels do not); and to this end, the apostle brings in these words prophesied of him, as spoken by him of himself, 'I will put my trust in him', as one proof that he was a man like unto us. Now for what was it that he trusted God? By the context it appears to be this, that he should be the salvation of his 'brethren' and 'children', and that he should have 'a seed and a generation to serve him', and raise up a church to God to praise him in. For this is made his confidence, and the issue of his sufferings, in that fore-cited Psa. 22, from verse 22 to the end.

Use. How should the consideration of these things both draw us on to faith, and encourage us therein, and raise up our hearts above all doubtings and withdrawings of spirit in believing! For in this example of Christ we have the highest instance of believing that ever was. He trusted God (as we have seen) for himself, and for many thousands besides, even for all his elect; and hast not thou the heart to trust him for one poor soul? Yea, Christ thus trusted God upon his single bond; but we, for our assurance, have both Christ and God bound to us, even God with his surety Christ (for he is God's surety as well as ours). A double bond from two such persons, whom would it not secure? If God the Father and God the Son thus mutually trusted one another for our salvation, whom would it not induce to trust them both, for one's own salvation, when as otherwise they must be damned that will not?

1. This example of Christ may teach and incite us to believe. For did Christ lay down all his glory, and empty himself, and leave himself worth nothing, but made a deed of surrendering all he had into his Father's hands, and this in a pure trust that God would 'justify many by him' (as it is in Isa. 53)? And shall not we lay down all we have, and part with whatever is dear unto us aforehand, with the

like submission, in a dependence and hope of being ourselves justified by him? And withal;—

2. It may encourage us to believe, especially against the greatness of sins. Hast thou the guilt of innumerable transgressions coming in and discouraging thee from trusting in him? Consider but what Christ had, though not of his own; Christ was made (as Luther boldly, in this sense that we speak of him, speaks),[1] the greatest sinner that ever was, that is, by imputation; for the sins of all God's chosen met in him. And yet he trusted God to be justified from them all, and to be raised up from under the wrath due to them. Alas! thou art but one poor sinner, and thy faith hath but a light and small load laid upon it, namely, thy own sins, which to this sum he undertook for, are but as an unit to an infinite number. 'God laid upon him the iniquities of us all.' Christ trusted God for his own acquittance from the sins of all the world, and when that was given him, he yet again further trusted him, to acquit the world for his satisfaction's sake.

But thou wilt say, Christ was Christ, one personally united to God, and so knew that he could satisfy him; but I am a sinful man. Well, but if thou believest, and so art one of those who are one with Christ, then Christ speaking these words in the name both of

[1] *Commentary on Galatians* (Gal. 3:13), *Tabletalk,* #202.—P.

himself and of his elect, as hath been showed, thou hast the very same ground to utter them that he had, and all that encouraged him may embolden thee, for he stood in thy stead. It was only thine and others' sins that put him in any danger of condemnation; and thou seest what his confidence beforehand was, that God would justify him from them all. And if he had left any of them unsatisfied for, he had not been justified; and, withal, in performing his own part undertaken by him, he performed thine also, and so in his being justified thou wert justified also. His confidence, then, may therefore be thine now; only his was in and from himself, but thine must be on him: yet so as by reason of thy communion with him in his both condemnation and justification, thou mayest take and turn all that emboldened him to this his trust and confidence, to embolden thee also in thine, as truly as he did for himself. Yea, in this thou hast now a farther prop and encouragement to thy faith, than he had; for now (when thou art to believe), Christ hath fully performed the satisfaction he undertook, and we now see Jesus crucified, acquitted, yea crowned with glory and honour, as the apostle speaks; but he, when he took up this triumph, was (as Isaiah here foretold and prophesied it of him), but as then entering upon that work. The prophet seeing the day of his arraignment and agony, utters these words as his; showing what thoughts should then possess his heart, when Pilate and the Jews should condemn him, and our sins come in upon him, 'God is near that justifies me; who therefore shall contend with me?' But now this comes to be added to *our* challenge here, that 'Christ *hath* died, and is also risen again'; that he *was* condemned and justified; who therefore shall condemn? may we say, and say much more.

But thou wilt yet say, He knew himself to be the Son of God, but so do not I. Well, do thou but cast thyself upon him, to be adopted and justified by him, with a giving up thy soul to his saving thee his own way, and, though thou knowest it not, the thing is done. And as for that so great and usual discouragement unto poor souls from doing this, namely, the greatness and multitudes of sins, this very example of his faith, and the consideration of it, may alone take off, and help to remove it, more than any I have ever met with; for he, in bearing the sins of his elect, did bear as great and infinitely more sins than thine, yea, all sorts of sins whatever, for some one of his elect or other, for he said upon it, that all (that is, all sorts of) sins shall be forgiven unto men, and therefore were first borne by him for them; and yet you see how confident aforehand he was, and is now clearly justified from them all. And by virtue of his being justified from all sorts of sins, shall all sorts of sinners in and through him be justified also; and, therefore, why mayest not thou hope to be from thine? Certainly for this very reason our sins, simply and alone considered, can be supposed no hindrance.

Thus we have met with one great and general encouragement at the very portal of this text, which comes forth to invite us ere we are entered into it, and which will await upon us throughout all that shall be said, and have an influence into our faith, and help to direct it in all that follows.

Chapter 2

The scope and argument of this discourse is, either direction to Christ as the object of faith, or encouragement to believers, from all those particulars in Christ mentioned in the text.

Faith and the supports of it, or rather Christ, as by his death and resurrection, *etc.*, he is the foundation of faith and the cause of our justification, is the main subject of these words. All which therefore, to handle more largely, is the intended subject of this

[Sect. 1]

discourse. And therefore, as we have seen Christ's faith for us, so now let us see what our faith is to be towards him: only take this along with you, for a right bounding of all that follows, that the faith (the object and support of which I would discourse of), is only faith *as justifying*; for justification was properly here the matter of Christ's faith for us, and is also answerably here held forth by Paul, as that faith which believers are to have on him. Now faith is called justifying, only as it hath justification for its object, and as it goes out to Christ for justification; so that all that shall be spoken must be confined to this alone, as the intendment of the text. And concerning this, the text doth two things:

1. It holds forth Christ the object of it, 'Who shall condemn? Christ hath died', *etc*. And he being the sole subject of those four particulars that follow, as encouragements to faith, must needs be therefore the object here set forth unto our faith.

2. In Christ we have here all those four things made matter of triumph to believers, to assure them they shall not be condemned, but justified: in that

Christ (1.) died, (2.) rose again, (3.) is at God's right hand, (4.) intercedes.

So that (for the general), I am to do two things; and therein I shall fulfil the text's scope.

1. *Direct your faith to Christ, as to its right object.*

2. *To encourage your faith from these several actions of Christ for us*, and show how they all contain matter of triumph for faith in them, and also teach your faith how to triumph from each of them. And herein I am to keep close to the argument propounded, namely, faith as justifying; or to show how faith, seeking justification in Christ, may be exceedingly raised from each of these particulars, and supported by them, as by so many pillars of it. So as although Christ's death, resurrection, *etc.*, may fitly serve to encourage our faith in many other acts it useth to put forth (as in point of sanctification to be had from Christ, into which his death and resurrection have an influence), yet here we are limited to the matter of justification only; 'It is God that justifies; who shall condemn, seeing Christ hath died?' and herein to show how his death, resurrection, *etc.*, may and do afford matter of comfort and triumphing in point of justification from all these. And thus you have the sum of these words, and of my scope in this ensuing treatise.

[Sect. 1]

Chapter 3

*First, Directions to Christ as the object of faith.—How in
a threefold consideration Christ is the object of justifying faith.*

But ere I come to encourage your faith from
these, let me first direct and point your faith aright
to its proper and genuine object, Christ. I shall do it
briefly, and only so far as it may be an introduction
to the encouragements from these four particulars,
the things mainly intended by me.

1. Christ is the object of our faith, in joint commission with God the Father.

2. Christ is the object of faith, in opposition to our
own humiliation, or graces, or duties.

3. Christ is the object of faith, in a distinction from
the promises.

1. First, Christ is the object of faith, in joint commission with God the Father. So here, 'it is God
that justifies', and 'Christ that died'. They are both
of them set forth as the foundation of a believer's
confidence. So elsewhere, faith is called a 'believing
on him [namely, God], that justifies the ungodly',
Rom. 4:5; and a 'believing on Christ', Acts 16:31.

Wherefore faith is to have an eye unto both, for both do alike contribute unto the justification of a sinner. It is Christ that paid the price, that performed the righteousness by which we are justified; and it is God that accepts of it, and imputes it unto us: therefore justification is ascribed unto both. And this we have in Rom. 3:24, where it is attributed unto them both together, 'Being justified freely by his grace, through the redemption that is in Jesus Christ.' Where we see that God's free grace and Christ's righteousness do concur to our justification. Christ paid as full a price, as if there were no grace shown in justifying us (for mercy bated[1] Christ nothing); and yet that it should be accepted for us, is as free grace, and as great as if Christ had paid never a farthing. Now as both these meet to justify us, so faith in justification is to look at both these. So it follows in the next verse, Rom. 3:25, 'Whom God hath set forth to be a propitiation, through faith in his blood.' And though it be true, that God justifying is the ultimate object of our faith, for Christ 'leads us by the hand' (as the word is, Eph. 2:18), 'unto God'; and in 1 Pet. 1:21, we are said 'by Christ to believe on God who raised him, that so our faith and hope might be on God';

---

[1] or *abated*: used here in the sense of reducing the price Christ had to pay to secure the justification of sinners. — P.

yet so, as under the New Testament, Christ is made the more immediate object of faith; for God dwelling in our nature is made more familiar to our faith than the person of the Father is, who is merely God. Under the Old Testament, when Christ was but in the promise, and not as then come in the flesh, then indeed their faith had a more usual recourse unto God, who had promised the Messiah, of whom they then had not so distinct, but only confused, thoughts; though this they knew, that God accepted and saved them through the Messiah. But now under the New Testament, because Christ as mediator exists not only in a promise of God's, but is come and manifest in the flesh, and is 'set forth by God' (as the apostle's phrase is), to transact all our business for us between God and us; hence the more usual and immediate address of our faith is to be made unto Christ; who as he is distinctly set forth in the New Testament, so he is as distinctly to be apprehended by the faith of believers. 'Ye believe in God' (saith Christ to his disciples, whose faith and opinion of the Messiah was till Christ's resurrection, of the same elevation with that of the Old Testament believers), 'believe also in me', John 14:1. Make me the object of your trust for salvation, as well as the Father. And, therefore, when faith and repentance come more narrowly to be distinguished by their more immediate objects, it is 'repentance towards God', but 'faith towards our Lord Jesus Christ', Acts 20:21; not that God and Christ are not the objects of both, but that Christ is more immediately the object of faith, and God of repentance: so that we believe in God through believing in Christ first, and turn to Christ by turning to God first. And this is there spoken, when they are made the sum of Christian doctrine, and of the apostles' preaching. And, therefore, the faith of some being much enlarged to the mercies of God and his free grace, and but in way of supposition unto Christ, or in a taking for granted that all mercies are communicated in and through Christ, yet so as their thoughts work not so much upon, nor are taken up about Christ; although this may be true faith under the New Testament, in that God and his free grace is the joint object of faith, together with Christ and his righteousness,—and the one cannot be without the other,—and God ofttimes doth more eminently pitch the stream of a man's thoughts in one channel rather than in another, and so may direct the course of a man's thoughts towards his free grace, when the stream runs less towards Christ, yet it is not such a faith as becomes the times of the gospel; it is of an Old Testament strain and genius; whereas our faith now should, in the more direct and immediate exercises of it, be pitched upon Jesus Christ, that 'through him', first apprehended, 'our faith might be in God' (as the ultimate object of it), as the apostle speaks, 1 Pet. 1:21. And so much for the first.

2. The second is, that Christ is to be the object of our faith, *in opposition to our own humiliation, or graces, or duties.*

(1.) We are not to trust, nor rest in humiliation, as many do, who quiet their consciences from this, that they have been troubled. That promise, 'Come to me, you that are weary and heavy laden, and you shall find rest', hath been much mistaken; for many have understood it, as if Christ had spoken peace and rest simply unto that condition, without any more ado, and so have applied it unto themselves, as giving them an interest in Christ; whereas it is only an invitement[1] of such (because they are most apt to be discouraged) to come unto Christ, as in whom alone their rest is to be found. If therefore men will set down their rest in being 'weary and heavy laden', and not come to Christ for it, they sit down besides Christ for it, they sit down in sorrow. This is to make John (who only prepared the way for Christ) to be the Messiah indeed (as many of the Jews thought),

[1] invitation. —P.

that is, to think the eminent work of John's ministry (which was to humble, and so prepare men for Christ) to be their attaining Christ himself. But if you be weary, you may have rest indeed, but you must come to Christ first. For as, if Christ had died only, and not arose, we had 'been still in our sins' (as it is 1 Cor. 15:17), so though we die by sin, as slain by it (as Paul was, Rom. 7:11-13, in his humiliation), yet if we attain not to the resurrection of faith (so the work of faith is expressed, Phil. 3:12, 13), we still remain in our sins.

(2.) Secondly, *we are not to rest in graces or duties*; they all cannot satisfy our own consciences, much less God's justice. If 'righteousness could have come' by these, then 'Christ had died in vain' (as Gal. 2:21). What a dishonour were it to Christ, that they should share any of the glory of his righteousness! Were any of your duties crucified for you? Graces and duties are the daughters of faith, the offspring of Christ; and they may in time of need indeed nourish their mother, but not at first beget her.

3. In the third place, *Christ's person, and not barely the promises of forgiveness, is to be the object of faith*. There are many poor souls humbled for sin, and taken off from their own bottom,[1] who, like Noah's

---

[1] resting place: foundation: grounds for confidence. —P.

dove, fly over all the word of God, to spy out what they may set their foot upon, and eying therein many free and gracious promises, holding forth forgiveness of sins, and justification, they immediately close with them, and rest on them alone, not seeking for, or closing with Christ in those promises. Which is a common error among people; and is like as if Noah's dove should have rested upon the outside of the ark, and not have come to Noah within the ark; where though she might rest for a while, yet could she not ride out all storms, but must needs have perished there in the end. But we may observe, that the first promise that was given, was not a bare word simply promising forgiveness, or other benefits which God would bestow; but it was a promise of Christ's person as overcoming Satan, and purchasing those benefits, 'The seed of the woman shall break the serpent's head.' So when the promise was renewed to Abraham, it was not a bare promise of blessedness and forgiveness, but of that seed, that is, Christ (as Gal. 3:16), in whom that blessedness was conveyed. 'In thy seed shall all the nations of the earth be blessed.' So that Abraham's faith first closed with Christ in the promise, and therefore he is said to see Christ's day, and to rejoice in embracing him. And so all the succeeding fathers (that were believers) did, more or less, in their types and sacraments, as appears by 1 Cor. 10:1, 2. And if they, then much more are we thus to look at Christ, unto whom he is now made extant, not in promises only, but is really incarnate, though now in heaven. Hence our sacraments (which are the seals added to the word of faith) do primarily exhibit Christ unto a believer, and so, in him, all other promises, as of forgiveness, *etc.*, are ratified and confirmed by them. Now there is the same reason of them, that there is of the promises of the gospel, for they preach the gospel to the eye, as the promise doth to the ear, and therefore as in them the soul is first to look at Christ, and embrace him as tendered in them, and then at the promises tendered with him in them, and not to take the sacraments as bare seals of pardon and forgiveness; so, in like manner, in receiving of, or having recourse to a promise, which is the word of faith, we are first to seek out for Christ in it, as being the foundation of it, and so to take hold of the promise in him. Hence faith is still expressed by this its object, Christ, it being called 'faith on Christ'. Thus Philip directs the eunuch Acts 8:35, 'Believe on the Lord Jesus.'

The promise is but the casket, and Christ the jewel in it; the promise but the field, and Christ the pearl hid in it, and to be chiefly looked at. The promises are the means by which you believe, not the things on which you are to rest. And so, although you are to look at forgiveness as held forth in the promise, yet you are to believe on Christ in that promise to obtain this forgiveness. So Acts 26:18, it is said of believers by Christ himself, 'that they may obtain forgiveness of sins, by faith which is on me'.

And to clear it farther, we must conceive, that the promises of forgiveness are not as the pardons of a prince, which merely contain an expression of his royal word for pardoning, so as we in seeking of it do rest upon, and have to do only with his word and seal, which we have to show for it; but God's promises of pardon are made in his Son, and are as if a prince should offer to pardon a traitor upon marriage with his child, whom in and with that pardon he offers in such a relation; so as all that would have pardon, must seek out for his child; and thus it is in the matter of believing. The reason of which is, because Christ is the *grand promise*, in whom 'all the promises are yea and amen', 2 Cor. 1:20, and therefore he is called the Covenant, Isa. 49:8. So that, as it were folly for any man to think that he hath an interest in an heiress's lands, because he hath got the writings of her estate into his hands, whereas the interest in the lands goes with her person, and with the relation of marriage to her, otherwise, without a title to herself, all the writings will be fetched out of his hands again; so is it with all the promises: they hang all upon Christ, and without him there is no interest to be had in them. 'He that hath the Son hath life', 1 John 5:12, because life is by God's appointment only in him, as verse 11. All the promises are as copyhold land, which when you would interest yourselves in, you inquire upon what lord it holds, and you take it up of him, as well as get the evidences and deeds for it into your hands; the lord of it will be acknowledged for such in passing his right into your hands. Now this is the tenure of all the promises; they all hold on Christ, in whom they are yea and amen; and you must take them up of him. Thus the apostles preached forgiveness to men, Acts 13:38, 'Be it known that through this man is preached to you the forgiveness of sins.' And as they preached, so we are to believe, as the apostle speaks, 1 Cor. 15:11. And without this, to rest on the bare promise, or to look to the benefit promised, without eying Christ, is not an evangelical, but a Jewish faith, even such as the formalists among the Jews had, who without the Messiah closed with promises, and rested in types to cleanse them, without looking unto Christ the end of them, and as propounded to their faith

[Sect. 1]

in them. This is to go to God without a mediator, and to make the promises of the gospel to be as the promises of the law, Nehushtan (as Hezekiah said of the brazen serpent),[1] a piece of brass, vain and ineffectual; like the waters of Bethesda, they heal not, they cleanse not, till this 'angel of the covenant' come down to your faith in them.[2] Therefore at a sacrament, or when you meet with any promise, get Christ first down by faith, and then let your faith propound what it would have, and you may have what you will of him.

There are three sorts of promises, and in the applying of all these, it is Christ that your faith is to meet with.

1. There are *absolute* promises, made to no conditions; as when Christ is said to 'come to save sinners', *etc.* Now in these it is plain, that Christ is the naked object of them; so that if you apply not him, you apply nothing, for the only thing held forth in them is Christ.

2. There are *inviting* promises; as that before mentioned, 'Come to me, you that are weary.' The promise is not to weariness, but to coming to Christ; they are bidden 'Come to him', if they will have rest.

---

[1] See 2 Kings 18:4.—P.
[2] See John 5:4.—P.

3. There are *assuring* promises; as those made to such and such qualifications of sanctification, *etc*. But still what is it that is promised in them, which the heart should only eye? It is Christ, in whom the soul rests and hath comfort in, and not in its grace; so that the sight of a man's grace is but a back door to let faith in at, to converse with Christ, whom the soul loves. Even as at the sacrament, the elements of bread and wine are but outward signs to bring Christ and the heart together, and then faith lets the outward elements go, and closeth, and treats immediately with Christ, unto whom these let the soul in; so grace is a sign inward, and whilst men make use of it only as of a bare sign to let them in unto Christ, and their rejoicing is not in it, but in Christ, their confidence being pitched upon him, and not upon their grace; whilst men take this course, there is and will be no danger at all in making such use of signs. And I see not, but that God might as well appoint his own work of the new creation within, to be as a sign and help to communion with Christ by faith, as he did those outward elements, the works of his first creation; especially, seeing in nature the effect is a sign of the cause. Neither is it more derogatory to free grace, or to Christ's honour, for God to make such effects signs of our union with him, than it was to make outward signs of his presence.

SECTION 2

CHRIST, THE OBJECT AND SUPPORT OF FAITH FOR JUSTIFICATION, IN HIS DEATH

Who shall condemn? Christ hath died.
ROM. 8:34.

Chapter 1

How not Christ's person simply, but Christ as dying, is the object of faith as justifying.

To come now to all these four particulars of or about Christ, as the object of faith here mentioned; and to show both how Christ in each is the object of faith as justifying; and what support or encouragement the faith of a believer may fetch from each of them in point of justification, which is the argument of the main body of this discourse.

First, Christ as dying is the object of justifying faith, 'Who shall condemn? Christ hath died.' For the explanation of which, I will

1. Give a direction or two.

2. Show how an encouragement, or matter of triumph, may from hence be fetched.

1. (1.) The first direction is this, that in seeking forgiveness or justification in the promises, as Christ is to be principally in the eye of your faith, so it must be Christ *as* crucified, Christ *as* dying, as here he is

made. It was the serpent as lift up, and so looked at, that healed them. Now this direction I give to prevent a mistake, which souls that are about to believe do often run into. For when they hear that the person of Christ is the main object of faith, they thus conceive of it, that when one comes first to believe, he should look only upon the personal excellencies of grace and glory which are in Jesus Christ, which follow upon the hypostatical union;[1] and so have his heart allured in unto Christ by them only, and close with him under those apprehensions alone. But although it be true, that there is that radical disposition in the faith of every believer, which if it were drawn forth to view Christ in his mere personal excellencies, abstractively considered, would close with Christ for them alone, as seeing such a beauty and suitableness in them; yet the first view which an humble soul always doth, and is to take of him, is of his being a Saviour, made sin, and a curse, and obeying to the death for sinners. He takes up Christ in his first sight of him, under the 'likeness of sinful flesh', Rom. 8:3, for so the gospel first represents him, though it holds forth his personal excellencies also; and in that representation it is that he is made a fit object for a sinner's faith to trust and

---

[1] The union of the divine nature and the human nature in the one person of the Lord Jesus Christ. — P.

rest upon for salvation; which in part distinguished a sinner's faith whilst here on earth, towards Christ, from that vision or sight which angels and the souls of men have in heaven of him. Faith here views him not only as glorious at God's right hand (though so also), but as crucified, as made sin, and a curse, and so rests upon him for pardon; but in heaven we shall 'see him as he is', and be made like unto him. Take Christ in his personal excellencies simply considered, and so with them propounded as an *head* to us, and he might have been a fit object for angels and men even without sin to have closed withal; and what an addition to their happiness would they have thought it, to have him for their husband! But yet, so considered, he should have been, and rather is, the object of love, than of faith or affiance.[1] It is therefore Christ that is thus excellent in his person, yet farther considered as clothed with his garments of blood, and the qualifications of a mediator and reconciler; it is this that makes him so desirable by sinners, and a fit object for their faith, which looks out for justification, to prey and seize upon, though they take in the consideration of all his other excellencies to allure their hearts to him, and confirm their choice of him.

[1] trust. — P.

Yea I say farther, that consider faith as justifying, that is, in that act of it which justifies a sinner; and so Christ, taken only or mainly in his personal excellencies, cannot properly be called the object of it. But the *formalis ratio*,[1] the proper respect or consideration that maketh Christ the object of faith as justifying, must necessarily be that in Christ, which doth indeed justify a sinner; which is, his obedience unto death. For the act and object of every habit or faculty are always suited, and similar each to other; and therefore Christ's justifying must needs be the object of faith justifying. It is true, that there is nothing in Christ with which some answerable act of faith in us doth not close; and from the differing considerations under which faith looks at Christ, have those several acts of faith various denominations: as faith that is carried forth to Christ and his personal excellencies may be called *uniting* faith; and faith that goes forth to Christ for strength of grace to subdue sin may, answerably to its object, be called *sanctifying* faith; and faith as it goes forth to Christ, as dying, *etc.*, for justification, may be called *justifying* faith. For faith in that act looks at what in Christ doth justify a sinner; and therefore Christ considered as dying, rising, *etc.*, doth in this respect become the most pleasing

---

[1] formal reason. — P.

and grateful object to a soul that is humbled; for this makes Christ suitable to him as he is a sinner, under which consideration he reflects upon himself, when he is first humbled. And therefore thus to represent Christ to believers under the law, was the main scope of all the sacrifices and types therein. 'All things being purged with blood, and without blood there being no remission', Heb. 9:22. Thus did the apostles also in their sermons. So Paul, in his Epistle to the Corinthians, seemed by the matter of his sermon to have 'known nothing but Christ, and him as crucified', 1 Cor. 2:2, as *Christ* above all, so Christ *as crucified* above all in Christ, as suiting their condition best, whom he endeavoured to draw on to faith on him. Thus, in his Epistle to the Galatians, he calls his preaching among them 'the preaching of faith', Gal. 3:2. And what was the main scope of it, but the picturing out (as the word is) of 'Christ crucified before their eyes'? verse 1. So he preached him, and so they received him, and so they 'began in the spirit', verse 3. And thus also do the seals of the promises (the sacraments) present Christ to a believer's eye; as they hold forth Christ (as was in the former direction observed), so Christ, *as crucified*; their scope being to 'show forth his death till he come', 1 Cor. 11:26, the bread signifying Christ's body broken in the sufferings of it; and the cup signifying the sufferings of his soul, and the pouring of it forth unto death. And hence likewise, as faith itself is called 'faith on Christ', as was before observed, so it is called 'faith on his blood', Rom. 3:25, because Christ, as shedding his blood for the remission of sins, is the object of it. So the words there are, 'whom God hath ordained to be a propitiation through faith in his blood, to declare his righteousness for the remission of sins'. And look how God hath ordained and set forth Christ in the promise: under that picture of him doth faith at first close with him. And one reason similar to the former may be grounded on the 24th verse of that 3rd to the Romans, 'Being justified freely by his grace, *through the redemption that is in Christ.*' And as I showed before, in the reason of the former direction, that all promises hold of his person, as being heir of all the promises; so the special tenure upon which forgiveness of sins doth hold of him is by purchase, and by the redemption that is in him. So that, as the promise of forgiveness refers to his person, so also to this redemption that is in him. Thus, both in Eph. 1:7 and Col. 1:14, 'In whom we have redemption through his blood, even the forgiveness of sins', his person gives us title to all the promises, and his blood shows the tenure they hold on; a purchase, and a full

price, ἀντίλυτρον [*antilutron*], and adequate price,
1 Tim. 2:6. And as sin is the strength of the law, and
of the threatenings thereof, so Christ's satisfaction
is the strength of all the promises in the gospel. In a
word, an humbled soul is to have recourse to that
Christ who is now alive and glorified in heaven, yet
to him as once crucified and made sin. He is to go
to Christ now glorified, as the person from whom
he is to receive forgiveness, *etc.*, but withal to him
as crucified; as through whom, considered in that
condition he then was in, he is to receive all.

Chapter 2

*What in Christ's death, faith seeking justification, is
especially to eye and look at.*

(2.) Now then a second direction for faith towards
Christ as dying, is, faith is principally and mainly to
look unto the end, meaning, and intent of God and
Christ in his sufferings, and not simply at the tragical
story of his death and sufferings. It is the heart, and
mind, and intent of Christ in suffering, which faith
chiefly eyeth, and which draweth the heart on to rest
on Christ crucified. When a believer sees that Christ's

aim in suffering for poor sinners agrees and answers to the aim and desires of his heart, and that that was the end of it, that sinners might have forgiveness, and that Christ's heart was as full in it, to procure it, as the sinner's heart can be to desire it; this draws his heart in to Christ, to rest upon him. And without this, the contemplation and meditation of the story of his sufferings, and of the greatness of them, will be altogether unprofitable. And yet all, or the chief use which the papists and many carnal protestants make of Christ's sufferings, is to meditate upon, and set out to themselves the grievousness of them, so to move their hearts to a relenting, and compassion to him, and indignation against the Jews for their crucifying of him, with an admiring of his noble and heroical love herein; and if they can but get their hearts thus affected, they judge and account this to be grace; whenas it is no more than what the like tragical story of some great and noble personage, full of heroical virtues and ingenuity, yet inhumanely and ungrately used, will work, and useth ordinarily to work in ingenuous[1] spirits, who read or hear of it, yea, and this ofttimes, though if it be but in the way of a fiction; which, when it reacheth no higher, is so far from being faith, that it is but a carnal and fleshly devotion,

---

[1] honourable, noble. — P.

springing from fancy, which is pleased with such a story, and the principles of ingenuity stirred towards one who is of a noble spirit, and yet abused. Such stories use to stir up a principle of humanity in men unto a compassionate love; which Christ himself at his suffering found fault with, as being not spiritual, nor raised enough, in those women who went weeping to see the Messiah so handled. 'Weep not for me', says he; that is, weep not so much for this, thus to see me unworthily handled by those for whom I die.[1]

And therefore, accordingly as these stirrings are but fruits of the flesh, so human inventions, as crucifixes, and lively representations of the story of Christ's passion unto the sight of fancy, do exceedingly provoke men to such devotional meditations and affections; but they work a bare historical faith only, a historical remembrance, and an historical love, as I may so call them. And no other than such doth the reading of the story of it in the word work in many, who yet are against such crucifixes. But saving, justifying faith chiefly minds, and is most taken up with the main scope and drift of all Christ's sufferings; for it is that in them which answers to its own aim and purpose, which is, to obtain forgiveness of sins in Christ crucified. As God looks principally at

[1] See Luke 23:27-31.—P.

the meaning of the Spirit in prayer, Rom. 8:27, so doth faith look principally to the meaning of Christ in his sufferings. As in all other truths a believer is said to have the mind of Christ, 1 Cor. 2:16, so especially he minds what was the mind and heart of Christ in all his sufferings. And therefore you may observe, that the drift of all the apostles' epistles, is to show the intent of Christ's sufferings; how he was therein set forth to be 'a propitiation for sin'; to 'bear our sins upon the tree'; to 'make our peace', *etc.*; 'he was made sin, that we might be made the righteousness of God in him'; as in like manner the scope of the Evangelists is to set forth the story of them, for that is necessary to be known also. And thus did that evangelical prophet Isaiah chiefly set forth the intent of Christ's sufferings for justification, Isa. 53, throughout the chapter, as David before had done the story of his passion, Psa. 22. And thus to show the use and purpose of his sufferings, was the scope of all the apostles' sermons, holding forth the intent of Christ's passion to be the justification and salvation of sinners. 'This is a faithful saying, and worthy of all acceptation, that Christ came into the world to save sinners', 1 Tim. 1:15; and they still set forth what the plot was, at which God by an ancient designment aimed at in the sufferings of Christ, which was an end higher than men or angels thought on, when he was put to death. And thus faith takes it up and looks at it. And upon this doth Peter (in his sermon, Acts 2) pitch their faith, where having set forth the heinousness of their sin in murdering 'the Lord of life', then to raise up their hearts again (that so seeing God's end in it, they might be drawn to believe), he tells them, that 'all this was done by the determinate counsel of God', verse 23, and that for a farther end than they imagined, even for the remission of sins through his name, as in the closure of that sermon he shows. It was not the malice of the Jews, the falseness of Judas, the fearfulness of Pilate, or the iniquity of the times he fell into, that wrought his death, so much as God his Father complotting with Christ himself, and aiming at a higher end than they did. There was a farther matter in it; it was the execution of an ancient contrivement and agreement, whereby God made Christ 'sin', and laid our sins upon him. God 'was in Christ, not imputing our sins to us, but making him sin', 2 Cor. 5:19-21. Which covenant Christ came, at his time, into the world to fulfil. 'Sacrifice and burnt offering thou wouldst not have', Heb. 10:5. 'Lo, I come to do thy will', and that will was 'to take away sins', verses 4, 10, 12, 14-16. These words Christ spake when he took our nature, and when he came into the world, clothed with infirmities like unto us sinners. 'God sent his Son in the likeness of sinful flesh, and for sin condemned sin in the flesh', Rom. 8:3. Mark that phrase 'for sin'; περι [*peri*] is there put for *propter*,[1] as John 10:33, οὐ περὶ καλου ἔργου [*ou peri kalou ergou*] 'not for a good work'. That is, not because of a good work, or for a good work's sake. So here, for sin, that is, because of sin. Sin was the occasion of his taking the likeness of sinful flesh. What, to increase it? No, but to condemn it, as it follows: that is, to cast and overthrow it in its power and plea against us, that instead of sin's condemning us, he might condemn sin, and that we might have 'the righteousness of the law', verse 5. This phrase 'for sin' is like unto that in Rom. 6:10, 'he died unto sin', that is, for sin's cause; for so the opposition that follows evinceth, 'In that he liveth, he liveth unto God', that is, for God and his glory. So he died merely for sin, that sin might have its course in justice, and for its sake suffered death, so putting to silence the clamour of it. The death of Christ was the greatest and strangest design that ever God undertook and acted, and therefore surely had an end proportionable unto it. God, that 'willeth not the death of a sinner', would not for

---

[1] Latin: *propter* = because. — P.

any inferior end will the death of his Son, whom he loved more than all creatures besides. It must needs be some great matter for which God should contrive the death of his Son, so holy, so innocent, and separate from sinners; neither could it be any other matter, than to destroy that which he most hated, and that was sin; and to set forth that which he most delighted in, and that was mercy. So Rom. 3:25, 26. And accordingly Christ demeaned himself in it, not at all looking at the Jews, or their malice, but at his Father's command and intent in it. And therefore when he was to arise to go unto that place where he should be taken, and carried to slaughter, 'As the Father gave me commandment', says he, 'so do I; arise, let us go hence', John 14:31. And when Judas went out at Christ's own provocation of him, 'What thou doest, do quickly', says he, 'the Son of man goeth as it was determined'; he looked to his Father's purpose in it. When he went out to be taken, it is said, 'Jesus knowing all things that should befall him, went forth', John 18:4. And when he was in his agony in the garden, whom doth he deal with but his Father? 'Father', he says, 'if it be possible, let this cup pass'; and God made his passion of so great necessity, that it was even impossible that that cup should pass. Indeed, had Christ stood in his own stead, it had been an easy request, yea, justice to grant it; and so he tells Peter, that he could command millions of angels to his rescue; but he merely submits unto his Father, 'Not my will, but thy will be done'; for God had laid upon him the iniquities of us all, Isa. 53.

Let our faith therefore look mainly to this design and plot of God, and of Christ in his suffering to satisfy for our sins, and to justify us sinners. When we consider him as born flesh and blood, and laid in a manger, think we withal that his meaning was to 'condemn sin in our flesh', Rom. 8:4. So when we read of him fulfilling all, or any part of righteousness, take we his mind in withal to be, that the 'law might be fulfilled in us', as it follows there, who were then represented in him, and so the fulfilling of it is accounted ours. Behold we him in his lifetime, as John the Baptist did, even as 'the Lamb of God, bearing and taking away the sins of the world'; and when upon the cross, let our faith behold the iniquities of us all met in him. 'Surely he hath borne our sorrows, bearing our sins in his body on the tree, and thereby once offered to bear the sins of many', Heb. 9, *etc.* This intent of Christ in all that he did and suffered, is that welcome news, and the very spirit of the gospel, which faith preys and seizeth on.

[Sect. 2]

Chapter 3

What support or matter of triumph Christ's death affords to faith for justification.

2. Now, having thus directed your faith to the right object, Christ, and Christ *as dying*; let us, secondly, see what matter of support and encouragement faith may fetch from Christ's death for justification. And surely that which hath long ago satisfied God himself for the sins of many thousand souls now in heaven, may very well serve to satisfy the heart and conscience of any sinner now upon earth, in any doubts in respect of the guilt of any sins that can arise. We see that the apostle here, after that large discourse of justification by Christ's righteousness, in the former part of this Epistle to the Romans, and having showed how every way it abounds, chapter 5, he now in this 8th chapter doth as it were sit down like a man over-convinced, as verse 31, 'What then shall we say to these things?' He speaks as one satisfied, and even astonished with abundance of evidence; having nothing to say, but only to admire God and Christ in this work; and therefore presently throws

down the gauntlet, and challengeth a dispute in this point with all comers. Let conscience and carnal reason, law and sin, hell and devils, bring in all their strength. 'Who is he shall lay any thing to the charge of God's elect?' 'Who shall condemn?' Paul dares to answer them all, and carry it with these few words, 'It is God that justifies, it is Christ that died.' And (as in verse 37) 'we are more than conquerors in all these'. It was this that brought in the prodigal, that in his 'father's house there was bread enough'. And so likewise he (whoever he was) who was the author of the 130th Psalm, when his soul was in deep distress by reason of his sins, verses 1-2, yet this was it that settled his heart to wait upon God, that there was 'plenteous redemption with him'. Christ's redemption is not merely ἀντίλυτρον [*antilutron*], a price or ransom equivalent, or making due satisfaction according to the just demerit of sin, but it is 'plenteous redemption'; there is an abundance of 'the gift of righteousness', Rom. 5:17, and 'unsearchable riches of Christ', Eph. 3:8. Yea, 1 Tim. 1:14, 'the grace of our Lord', that is, of Christ, as verse 12, ὑπερεπλεόνασε [*huperepleonase*], we translate it, 'was abundant', but the word reacheth farther, 'it was overfull, redundant, more than enough'. And yet (says Paul, verse 13) I had sins enough to pardon, as one would think, that might exhaust it, 'I was a blasphemer', *etc.* But I found so much grace in Christ, even more than I knew what to do withal.

I shall not insist so largely on this first head of Christ's dying, as upon those three following, because it is the main subject of another discourse, which, through God's grace, I intend to publish, though in another method.[1] Only, for a taste, to instance in some few particulars, showing how Christ's satisfaction may be opposed, and set against the guilt of a poor sinner's offences. What is there that can be said to aggravate sin in the general, or any man's particular sins, that may not be answered out of this, 'Christ hath died'? and something be considered in it, which the conscience may oppose thereto? So that whatever evil, which according to the rules of spiritual reason (which the righteous law proceedeth by, and containeth as the foundation of its righteousness in condemning or aggravating sin), a man's conscience may suggest to be in sin; oppositely hereunto may a man's faith, according to the like rules of true spiritual reason, show a more transcendent goodness to

[1] Most probably a reference to *A Discourse of Christ the Mediator*, originally published posthumously by Goodwin's son in *The Works of Thomas Goodwin, D.D.*, vol. 3, 1692, and in vol. 5 of the Nichol edition, 1863. It is an extensive treatment of all aspects of Christ's death. —P.

have been in Christ's death, which the gospel reveals, and so many oppose the one to the other, and have as good reason to show why sin should not condemn, from Christ's death, as conscience can have, that the law may condemn.

(1.) As first, is sin the transgression of the law? Christ dying, the law-maker, was subjected to the law; and will not that make amends? Is sin the debasement of God's glory, manifested in his word and works? Christ's dying was the debasement and emptying of the brightness of his glory in the highest measure, who was God personally manifested in the flesh. The one of them is but as the darkening the shine or lustre of the sun upon a wall, but the other is as the obscuring of the sun itself. Sin's highest evil lies in offending God, but Christ's righteousness is (oppositely) the righteousness of God himself, or Jehovah made our righteousness. So that God in our sin is considered but as the object against whom; but God in this our righteousness, is the subject from whom and in whom this righteousness comes and is seated. And so his Godhead answerably gives a higher worth to it, by how much the alliance which the subject hath to an action of its own, that proceeds from it, is nearer than that which an object hath, against which the action is committed.

(2.) Or secondly, what peculiar aggravations or circumstances are there in thy sins, to weigh thee down, with which some circumstances in Christ's obedience and death may not be paralleled, to lift thee up again?

As *first*, is it the greatness of thy sin in the substance of the fact committed? Hath there been lewdness in thy wickedness, as the prophet speaks? [cf. Ezek. 23; 24:13]. Consider what guilt, of how heinous crimes, God suffered to be laid to Christ's charge by profane men, when he was made an offering for sin. He died as a traitor to his prince, and a blasphemer of God in the highest kind of blasphemy, as making himself equal with God; an impostor, a seducer, yea, a devil, yea, a prince of devils, than whom a murderer was esteemed more worthy to live. Which imputations, though by men unjustly charged on him, yet by God were so ordered as just, in respect of his bearing our sins. For him who was holiness itself to be made the greatest of sinners, yea, to be 'made sin', and the worst of sins, and accordingly to suffer from God and men, what greater satisfaction for the taking of sins away can be desired or imagined?

Or *secondly*, dost thou aggravate thy sins by the naughtiness of thy heart in sinning, and sayest that the inward carriage thereof hath been much worse than the outward? Look thou into the heart of Jesus Christ dying, and behold him struggling with his Father's wrath, thou wilt find the sufferings of his soul more than those of his body, and in them to lie the soul of his sufferings.

Thirdly, may thy sin be aggravated, in that thou didst commit it with so great delight and greediness, and pouredst out thy heart unto it? Consider that Christ offered himself more willingly than ever thou didst sin. 'Lo, I come', says he, Psa. 40, 'I delight to do thy will'; and 'how am I straitened till it be accomplished!' Luke 12:50. And though to show how great an evil and misery it was in itself, he showed an averseness to it; yet as it was his Father's will for our salvation, he heartily embraced and drank off that cup unto the bottom.

Fourthly, didst thou sin with much deliberation, when thou mightest have avoided it? There was in this circumstance in Christ's sufferings to answer that, that he knew all he was to suffer, and yet yielded up himself, as John 18:4.

Fifthly, hast thou sinned presumptuously, and made a covenant with death and hell? Christ in like manner offered up himself by a covenant and complot with his Father so to do.

Sixthly, are there any especial circumstances of time and place, *etc.*, that aggravate thy sins?

As first, that so great a person in the church should scandalize the name of God in sinning. Why, how great a person was Christ? Even equal with God the Father; and yet how greatly humbled, even to the death; his offices of King, Priest, and Prophet being debased with him. How great a name had he! as Heb. 1:4, which notwithstanding was dishonoured more than ever any man's.

Or secondly, that thou sinnedst at such a time, or in such a company, which sometimes serve to make a sin the more heinous. Consider how God contrived to have the shame and affliction of his Son's death aggravated by all these circumstances. It was of deaths the most accursed, at a time most solemn, in a place most infamous, with company most wretched.

Thus might we find out that in Christ's suffering and satisfaction made, that would fitly answer to anything in our sins; and so thereby we should be the more relieved. And though the whole body of his sufferings do stand and answer for the whole bulk of our sinnings, yet the consideration of such particulars will much conduce to the satisfying of an humbled and dejected soul, about the particulars of its sinnings.

Therefore (to conclude) get your hearts and consciences distinctly and particularly satisfied in the
all-sufficiency of worth and merit which is in the
satisfaction that Christ hath made. As it is a fault and
defect in humiliation, that men content themselves
with a general apprehension and notion that they are
sinners, and so never become thoroughly humbled; so
it is a defect in their faith, that they content themselves
with a superficial and general conceit, that Christ
died for sinners, their hearts not being particularly
satisfied about the transcendent all-sufficiency of his
death. And thence it is, that in time of temptation,
when their abounding sinfulness comes distinctly to
be discovered to them, and charged upon them, they
are then amazed and their faith nonplussed, as not
seeing that in Christ which might answer to all that
sinfulness. But as God saw that in Christ's death which
satisfied him, so you should endeavour by faith to see
that worth in it which may satisfy God, and then your
faith will sit down as satisfied also. If a man were to
dispute for his life some hard and difficult controversy,
wherein are many great and strong objections to be
taken away, he would be sure to view, and study, and
ponder all that might be said on that other part which
he were to hold, in way of answer to them, and to get
such a clear and convincing light as might make the

truth of his position apparent and manifest through those clouds of objections that hang in the way. Now you will all be thus called one day to dispute for your souls, sooner or later; and therefore such skill you should endeavour to get in Christ's righteousness, how in its fullness and perfection it answereth to all your sinfulness; that your hearts may he able to oppose it against all that may be said of any particular, in or about your sins; that in all the conflicts of your spirits, you may see that in it which would clear your whole score; and that if God would but be pleased to impute it to you, you might say, I durst presently come to an account with him, and cut scores with his law and justice.

Thus much of the first thing made the object of faith, namely, Christ *as dying*.

SECTION 3

FAITH SUPPORTED BY CHRIST'S RESURRECTION

… yea rather, that is risen again.
ROM. 8:34.

Chapter 1

Christ's resurrection supporteth faith two ways: 1. By being an evidence of our justification; 2. By having an influence into our justification.—The necessity of Christ's resurrection, for the procuring our justification.

The next thing to be looked at in Christ, as he is the object of justifying faith, and from whence our faith may seek and fetch support and comfort in the matter of justification, is Christ's resurrection: upon which we see here, the apostle putteth a *rather*, 'Yea rather, that is risen again.' There must therefore be some special thing in the resurrection of Christ, which it contributes to our faith and justification, for which it should have a *rather* put upon it, and that comparatively to his death. Now to show wherein this should lie, consider how the resurrection of Christ serveth to a double use and end, in the matter of justification.

First, as an *evidence* to our faith, that God is fully satisfied by Christ's death; his resurrection may give us full assurance of it.

Secondly, it had, and hath an *influence* into our justification itself; yea, and as great an influence as his death had. In both these respects it deserves a *rather* to be put upon it, and Paul had them both in his eye, when he wrote these words. So as first, if you ask an account of his faith, and a reason of his so triumphant assurance, he allegeth his resurrection to confirm it, 'Christ is risen.' Or,

Secondly. If you would have a reason of the thing, how it comes to pass that we who are believers cannot be condemned; 'Christ is risen', saith he. He allegeth it as a cause, that hath such an influence into justification itself, as it makes all sure about it.

1. By way of evidence. Although Christ's obedience in his life and his death past do alone afford the whole matter of our justification, and make up the sum of that price paid for us (as hath been shown), so as faith may see a fullness of worth and merit therein, to discharge the debt; yet faith hath a comfortable sign and evidence to confirm itself in the belief of this, from Christ's resurrection after his death. It may fully satisfy our faith, that God himself is satisfied, and that he reckons the debt as paid. So that our faith may boldly come to God, and call for the bond in, as having Christ's resurrection to show for it, that the debt is discharged. And hence the

apostle cries *victory* over sin, hell, and death, upon occasion of, and as the *coronis* and conclusion of that, his large discourse about Christ's resurrection, 1 Cor. 15:55-57, 'O death, where is thy sting?' that is, sin, and the power of it; for so it follows, 'the sting of death is sin'; and 'O grave, where is thy victory? Thanks be to God who hath given us victory, through Jesus Christ our Lord', namely, as risen again; for of his resurrection, and of that chiefly, had he spoken throughout that chapter.

2. But surely this is not all, that it should only argue our justification by way of evidence. This alone would not have deserved such a *rather* to be put upon it, if Christ's resurrection had not had some farther real causal influence into justification itself, and been more than simply an evidence of it to our apprehensions. Therefore, secondly, in justification, although the *materiale*, or matter of it, be wholly the obedience and death of Christ; yet the act of pronouncing us righteous by that his obedience (which is the *formale* of justification), doth depend upon Christ's resurrection. Ordinarily there hath been no more expressed concerning this dependence, than that the resurrection of Christ justifies by working actual faith, to lay hold upon what Christ hath done in his life and death, which is called the applying

of it, of which more anon. But that speech of Paul, 1 Cor. 15:17, seems to import more, 'If Christ be not risen again, ye are yet in your sins, and your faith is in vain'; that is, although you could suppose faith to be wrought in you upon the merit of Christ's dying, yet it would be in vain if Christ were not risen again; for your title to justification itself would be void; 'you were yet in your sins'. Which is said, because his resurrection was it, whereby sins (though satisfied for in his death) were taken off, and they acquitted from them; which I take to be the meaning also of that, Rom. 4:25, 'He was delivered for our sins, and rose again for our justification.' When the apostle says, 'for our sins he was delivered', he means his laying down that which was the price for them, a satisfaction for them, which his death was. And in that sense, 'he died for our sins'; that is, his death stands instead of our death, and so satisfies for sin. But yet still that upon which the act of God's justifying us, and his discharge given us from our sins, and whereby he reckoneth us justified, that depends upon his resurrection. 'He rose again for our justification.' Note that justification there imports the act of imputation, and reckoning us just, which he had spoken of in the verses immediately foregoing, verses 22-24. In a word, to the full discharge of a debt, and freeing the debtor, two things are requisite: 1. The payment of the debt; 2. The tearing or cancelling of the bond, or receiving an acquittance for the freeing of the debtor. Now the payment was wrought by Christ's death, and the acquittance to free from the death was at and by his resurrection.

Chapter 2

For the explanation of both these is shown, how Christ sustained a double relation first, of a surety given for us; secondly, of a common person in our stead. The difference of these two, and the usefulness of these two considerations, for the explaining all the rest that follows, in this whole discourse.

Now the better to explicate both these, you must consider how that Christ, in almost all that he did *for us* (as the phrase is here, and is to be annexed to each particular) did stand in a double relation for us unto God.

1. Of a *surety*, bound to pay the debt for us, and to save our souls.

2. Of a *common person*, or as an attorney-at-law in our stead. And both these, as they have a distinct

and differing consideration in themselves, so those several considerations of them will conduce to the understanding of those two things forementioned, as ways and arguments to show how the resurrection of Christ may support our faith, both by way of *evidence* that the debt is paid, and by way of *influence* that we are thereby acquitted, and cannot be condemned. The notion of his being risen, who is our surety, clears the first, and that of his rising as a common person, illustrates the other. And I shall here a little the largelier insist upon the explication of these two relations, because their consideration will be of use through all the rest that follows, to illustrate thereby the influence that his ascension, and sitting at God's right hand, *etc.*, have into our justification; and so I shall carry them along throughout this discourse.

1. A surety is one that undertakes, and is bound to do a thing for another; as to pay a debt for him, or to bring him safe to such or such a place, or the like; so as when he hath discharged what he undertook and was bound for, then the party for whom he undertook is discharged also.

2. A common person with, or for another he goes for, is one who represents, personates, and acts the part of another, by the allowance and warrant of the law; so as what he doth, as such a common person,

and in the name of the other, that other whom he personates is by the law reckoned to do; and, in like manner, what is done to him, as being in the other's stead and room, is reckoned as done to the other. Thus, by our law, an attorney appears for another, and money received by him is reckoned as received by him whom it is due unto. Thus the giving possession of an estate, a re-entry made, and possession taken of land, *etc.*, if done by and to a man who is his lawful attorney, it stands as good in law unto a man, as if in his own person it had been done. So ambassadors for princes represent their masters: what is done to them is reckoned as done to the prince; and what they do, according to their commission, is all one as if the prince, whose person they represent, had done it himself. In like manner also, the marriages of princes are transacted and solemnized by proxy, as a common person representing his lord, and in his name, is married to a princess in her father's court; and the laws of men authorize it, and the marriage is as good as if both princes themselves had been present, and had performed all the rites of it. And thus to be a common person is more than simply to be a surety for another: it is a farther thing; and therefore these two relations are to be distinctly considered, though they seem to be somewhat of a like nature. Thus an attorney is a different thing from a surety. A surety undertakes to pay a debt for another, or the like; but a common person serves to perform any common act, which by the law is reckoned and virtually imputed to the other, and is to stand as the other's act, and is as valid as if he had done it; so as the good and benefit which is the consequent of such an act, shall accrue to him whom he personated, and for whom he stood as a common person. Adam was not a surety for all mankind; he undertook not for them in the sense forementioned, but he was a common person representing all mankind; so as what he should do was to be accounted as if they had done it. Now the better to express and make sure our justification in and by Christ, according to all sorts of laws (the equity of all which God usually draws up into his dispensations), God did ordain Christ both to be a surety for us, and also a common person representing us, and in our stead. That as Christ took all other relations for us, as of an Husband, Head, Father, Brother, King, Priest, Captain, *etc.* that so the fullness of his love might be set forth to us, in that what is defective in any one of these relations, is supplied and expressed by the other; even thus did God ordain Christ to take and sustain both these relations, of a surety and a common person, in all he did for us, thereby to make our justification by him the more full and legal; and justify, as I may so speak, our justification itself or his justifying of us, by all sorts of legal considerations whatever, that hold commonly among men in like case; and that which the one of these relations or considerations might not reach to make good, the other might supply; what fell short in the one the other might make up; and so we might be most legally and formally justified, and made sure never to be condemned.

Chapter 3

The first head: The evidence of justification which Christ's resurrection affords to faith, explained by two things.
1. By showing how Christ was made a Surety for us.
2. How his resurrection as a Surety holds forth this evidence.

1. Concerning the first of those two heads at first propounded, namely, the evidence which Christ's resurrection affords unto our faith in point of noncondemnation, I have two things to handle in this chapter to make this out: First, how Christ was made a Surety for us, and what manner of Surety he did

become; secondly, what the consideration hereof will contribute to that evidence which faith hath from Christ's resurrection.

(1.) For the first, Christ was appointed by God (and himself also undertook) to be our Surety. This you have, Heb. 7:22, 'He was made Surety of a better testament' or covenant, namely, of the new. The Hebrew word for *covenant* the Septuagint still translated Διαθήκη [*Diatheke*] *testament*: the word in the Hebrew being of a large signification, and comprehending both a covenant and testament; and so in the New Testament it is used promiscuously for either; and indeed this 'new covenant of grace' is both. Of this covenant Christ is the ἔγγυος [*enguos*], the plighter of his troth for it, the Surety, the Promiser, the Undertaker. The verb this comes of is ἐγγυάω [*enguao*], *promittere*, which comes from ἐν γυίοις [*en guiois*], *in manibus*, striking hands, or giving one's hand, as a sign of a covenant; and so to bargain with, or make up a covenant. 'Be not thou one of them that strike hands, or of them that are sureties for debts', Prov. 22:26: which whole verse the Septuagint reads, Give not thyself εἰς ἐγγύην [*eis enguen*], *to suretyship*; the same word that is here used by the apostle. It was the manner both of the Jews and Romans also, to make covenants by striking of hands. And in testaments, the heir and executor shook hands, or the executor gave his hand to fulfil it. And the word ἐγγυήσασθαι [*enguesasthai*] is used, not only in promising to pay a debt for another, but also in becoming a pledge for another, for to undergo death or a capital punishment in another's room, as in that famous story of friends, namely, Evephenus and Eucritus: Eucritus did ἠξίωσεν ἐγγυήσασθαι [*exiosen enguesasthai*],[1] willingly become a surety for Evephenus, when condemned to die by Dionysius the tyrant. This very word is used by Polyænus,[2] the historian of that fact. Now such a *Surety* every way did Christ become unto God for us, both to pay the debt, by undergoing death in our stead, and so to satisfy God; and then as the *Heir*, to execute his will and testament. He became a Surety of the whole covenant, and every condition in it, take it in the largest sense; and this of all, both on God's part, and on ours. For us he undertook to God to work all our works, and undergo all our punishments; to pay our debts for

---

[1] It is remarkable that Goodwin has, through inadvertence, mistaken the meaning of this expression. It was Evephenus, who, having sent for Eucritus, ἠξίωσεν ἐγγυήσασθαι, asked him to stand surety for him. The mistake does not affect the argument, which depends upon the meaning of ἐγγυήσασθαι, and not upon that of ἠξίωσεν. —Ed.

[2] *Strategems*, Book 5 chap. 2. —Ed.

us, and to work in us all that God required should be done by us, in the covenant of grace. And thus to be a surety is much more than simply to be an intercessor or mediator (as Pareus well observes). God did (as it were) say to Christ, What they owe me, I require it all at your hands; and Christ assented, and from everlasting struck hands with God, to do all for us that God could require, and undertook it under the penalty that lay upon us to have undergone.

Yea, Christ became such a Surety in this for us, as is not to be found among men. On earth, sureties are wont to enter into one and the same bond with the debtors, so as the creditor may seize on which of the two he will, whether on the debtor or on the surety, and so (as usually) on the debtor first, for him we call the principal. But in this covenant God would have Christ's single bond; and hence Christ is not only called the Surety of the covenant for us, but 'the Covenant', Isa. 49:8, and elsewhere. God making the covenant of grace primarily with him, and with him as for us, thereby his single bond alone was taken for all, that so God might be sure of satisfaction: therefore he laid all upon Christ, protesting that he would not deal with us, nor so much as expect any payment from us, such was his grace. So Psa. 89:19, where the mercies of the covenant made between

Christ and God, under the type of God's covenant with David, are set forth, 'Thou spakest in vision to thy holy One, and saidst, I have laid help on one who is mighty.' As if God had said, I know that these will fail me, and break, and never be able to satisfy me; but you are a mighty and substantial person, able to pay me, and I will look for my debt of you. And to confirm this, than which nothing can give stronger consolation, or more advanceth God's free grace, when God went about the reconciling the world in and by Christ, and dealt with Christ about it, the manner of it is expressed to have been, that God took off our sins from us, and discharged us, as it were, meaning never to call us to an account for them, unless Christ should not satisfy him, and laid them all on Christ, so as he would require an account of them all from him first, and let him look to it; and this he did to make the covenant sure. Thus, 2 Cor. 5:19, it is said (the apostle speaking of God's transaction of this business with Christ) that 'God was in Christ', namely, from everlasting, 'reconciling the world' (of elect believers) 'to himself, not imputing their trespasses to them; and made him sin who knew no sin.' Observe, that as he laid our sins on Christ, so withal he discharged us in his compact between Christ and himself, 'not imputing their trespasses to them'. So then, all laid upon Christ, and he was to look to it, or else his soul was to have gone for it. This is not the manner of other creditors: they use to charge the debt on both the surety and the debtor; but in this covenant (of grace, namely) Christ's single bond is entered; he alone is 'the Covenant', so as God will have nought to say to us, till Christ fails him. He hath engaged himself first to require satisfactions at Christ's hands, who is our Surety.

(2.) Now then for to make use of this notion, for the clearing of the point in hand. It might afford us matter of unspeakable comfort, only to hear of Christ's having been arrested by God for our debt, and cast into prison, and his bond sued, and an execution or judgment served on him, as the phrases are, Isa. 53:8. For thereby we should have seen how God had begun with our Surety, as minded to let us alone, and that it lay on him to discharge the debt, who was so able to do it. And thereby we might also see how he was 'made sin for us', and therefore we might very well have quieted our hearts from fearing any arrests, or for God's coming upon us, till we should hear that our surety were not sufficiently able to pay the debt, as you have heard he is.

But yet our hearts would still be inquisitive (for all that) to hear whether indeed he hath perfectly

[Sect. 3]

satisfied God or no; and would be extremely solicitous to know whether he hath satisfactorily performed what he undertook, and how he got clear of that engagement, and of being 'made sin for us'. And therefore the apostle comforts believers with this, that Christ shall 'the next time appear without sin'. 'Unto them that look for him he shall appear the second time, without sin, unto salvation', Heb. 9:28. One would think it no great matter of comfort to us to hear that Christ should appear without sin; for who would imagine that it could be otherwise with 'the Holy One', 'the Lord of glory'? There is no wonder in that. Ay, but, says the apostle, your very salvation is interested in this, as nearly as is possible. It is well for you that Christ is now without sin; for he having as your Surety undertook to satisfy for sin, and having accordingly been once made sin when on earth, and arrested for it by God at his death; in that now he is got clear of that engagement—which could be no way but by satisfaction, which he undertook—this doth plainly evince it, and ascertain you, that you shall never be condemned for it; for by the law, if the surety hath discharged the debt, the debtor is then free. And therefore no news would or could be more welcome to sinners, than to have a certain and infallible evidence given, that their Surety were well come off, and had quitted all, to satisfaction.

Now then to evidence this serveth his resurrection; 'Christ is risen.' Nothing so sure. Therefore certainly the debt is discharged, and he hath paid it to the full, and so is now without our sin, and fully got clear of it. For God having once arrested Christ, and cast him into prison, and begun a trial against him, and had him to judgment, he could not come forth till he had paid the very utmost farthing. And there is the greatest reason for it, to ascertain us, that can be. For he was under those bonds and bolts, which if it had 'been possible', would have 'detained' him in the grave, as Acts 2:24. The strength of sin, and God's wrath, and the curse against sin (thou shalt die the death) did as cords hold him, as the psalmist's phrase is. Other debtors may possibly break their prisons; but Christ could not have broke through this, for the wrath of the all-powerful God was this prison, from which there was no escaping, no bail; nothing would be taken to let him go out but full satisfaction. And therefore to hear that Christ is risen, and so is come out of prison, is an evidence that God is satisfied, and that Christ is discharged by God himself; and so is now 'without sin', walking abroad again at liberty. And therefore the apostle proclaims a mighty victory, obtained by Christ's resurrection, over death, the grave, the strength of sin, the law, 1 Cor. 15:55, 56, and cries out, 'Thanks be to God, who giveth us the victory, through Jesus Christ our Lord', verse 57. You may now rest secure indeed: 'Christ is risen; who therefore shall condemn?'

Chapter 4

The second head propounded, the influence Christ's resurrection hath into justification. — Two branches of the demonstration of this: First, that Christ was a common person, representing us in all he was, or did, or suffered, handled at large; more especially a common person in his resurrection.

2. Now secondly, to come to that other head propounded, the influence Christ's resurrection hath into our justification. The demonstration or making out of which depends on two things put together; the first, how Christ was appointed by God, and himself acted the part of a common person, representing us in what he did, and more particularly in his resurrection. Of this in this chapter.

The second is, how from that consideration ariseth, not only an evidence to our faith, but a real influence into our justification and non-condemnation. So as, 'Who shall condemn?' because 'Christ is risen again', as a common person, representing us therein.

(1.) For the first of these, to illustrate and prove it in the general, that instance of Adam serves most fitly, and is indeed made use of in the Scripture to that end. Adam, as you all know, was reckoned as a common public person, not standing singly or alone for himself, but as representing all mankind to come of him. So as by a just law, what he did was reckoned to his posterity whom he represented. And what was by that law threatened, or done to him for what he did, is threatened against his posterity also. Now this man was herein a lively type of our Lord Christ, as you have it, 'who was the type of him who was to come', Rom. 5:14. Unto which purpose, the titles which the apostle gives these two, Christ and Adam, 1 Cor. 15:47, are exceeding observable; he calls Adam 'the first man'; and Christ our Lord, 'the second man'; and both for that very purpose and respect which we have in hand. For, first, he speaks of them as if there had never been any more men in the world, nor were ever to be for time to come, except these two. And why? but because these two between them had all the rest of the sons of men hanging at their girdle; because they were both common persons, that had the rest in like (though opposite) considerations included and involved in them. Adam had all the sons of men, born into this world, included in himself, who are therefore called 'earthly men', verse 48, in a conformity to him 'the earthly man', verse 47; and Christ the second man had all his elect—who are 'the first born', and whose 'names are written in heaven', and therefore, in the same verse, are oppositely called 'heavenly men'—included in him. You see how he sums up the number of all men in two, and reckons but two men in all; these two, in God's account, standing for all the rest. And farther observe, that because Adam was in this his being a common person unto us, the shadow and the lively type of Christ, who was to come after him; that therefore he is called 'the first man' of these two, and Christ 'the second man', as typified out by him.

Now if you ask wherein Christ was a common person, representing us, and standing in our stead; I answer, if in anything, then in all those conditions and states wherein he was, in what he did, or befell him, whilst here on earth especially. For he had no other end to come down into this world, but to sustain our persons, and to act our parts, and to have what was to have been done to us acted upon him.

[1.] Thus, first, in their two several conditions,

qualifications, and states, they both were common persons. That is, look what state or condition the one or the other was made in, is by a just law to be put upon those whom they represented. So the apostle reasons from it, verse 48, 'as is the earthly man' (namely, the first man, Adam), 'such are the earthly', namely, to be earthly men as well as he; because he who is a common person representing them, was in his condition but an earthly man. And oppositely, by the same law, it follows, 'as is the heavenly man' (namely, the second man, Christ), 'such are and must be the heavenly', who pertain to him, because he also is a common person, ordained to personate them; and Adam, who came after him, was therein but his type.

[2.] And as thus, in this place to the Corinthians, the apostle argues Christ to be a common person, in respect of his condition and state, by an argument of parallels taken from his type, Adam; so, secondly, in that 5th to the Romans, he argues Christ to have been a common person, in his actions which he did on earth: and this also from the similitude of Adam, whom, Rom. 5:14, he therein makes to have been Christ's type. And he speaks of Adam there as a common person, both in respect of what he did, namely, his *sin*; and also in respect of what befell him for his sin, namely, *death* and condemnation. And because he was in all these not to be considered as a *single man*, but as one that was *all men*, by way of representation; hence, both what he did, they are said to do in him; and what condemnation or death was deserved by his sin, fell upon them all, by this law of his being a public person for them.

First, For what he did. He sinned, you know, and, verse 12, all are said to have sinned, namely, in his sin; yea, and according to those words in the Greek, ἐν ᾧ [*en ho*],[1] which are added there, you may render that sentence (and the original bears it, and it is also varied in the margin) thus, 'in whom all have sinned', namely, in Adam, as in a public person. Their act was included in his, because their persons were included in his. And

Secondly, For what befell him for sin, that befell them also by the same law of his being a person representing them. Hence, verse 12, death is said to

[1] This reading, ἐν ᾧ, for ἐφ' ᾧ, which the author quotes, and which our translators must have had before them, is not given by Griesbach.—Ed. It is indeed strange that Goodwin should speak of the Greek of Rom. 5:12 as ἐν ᾧ [*en ho*], for which there is no apparent manuscript evidence. Presumably Goodwin knew that in the old Latin rendering followed by Augustine and others the translation read *in quo* (= in whom), which may reflect the fact that these early translators were working with a text saying ἐν ᾧ [*en ho*]. However that may be, this translation affected Augustine's understanding of the text, and that is followed by Goodwin here.—P.

'pass upon all men', namely, for this, that Adam's sin was considered as theirs, as it there follows. It is said to pass, even as a sentence of death passeth upon a condemned malefactor. And, verse 18, judgment is said to 'come by that one man's offence, upon all men, to condemnation'. Now in Genesis 2:17, the threatening was spoken only to Adam, as but one man, 'In the day that thou eatest thereof, thou shalt surely die.' And Genesis 3:19, that sentence seems only to pass upon him alone, 'Unto dust thou shalt return.' Yet in threatening Adam, God threatened us all; and in sentencing Adam to death, he sentenced us also. The curse reacheth us too; 'death passed upon all men' then, and therefore by a just law 'death reigns over all', as Rom. 5:14 and 17, because Adam was in all this a common person representing us, and so in our stead; and so all this concerns us as truly and as nearly as it did him. I say by a just law; for, indeed, the Scripture, upon the equity of this rule, pronounceth a statute out against all men that they should die, Heb. 9:27. *Statutum est*, it is appointed by a statute law that all should die. Now if you search for this statute, when and where enacted, you will find that the original record and roll is that in Genesis 3:19, spoken only of Adam, but holding true of us, 'to dust thou shalt return'.

(3.) Just thus the matter stands in the point of our justification and salvation between Christ and elect believers; for Adam was herein his type. Christ was considered and appointed of God as a common person, both in what he did and in what was done to him. So as by the same law, what he did for us is reckoned or imputed to us, as if we ourselves had done it; and what was done to him, tending to our justification and salvation, is reckoned as done to us. Thus when Christ died, he died as a common person, and God reckoneth that we died also. When Christ arose, he rose as our head, and as a common person, and so then God accounts that we rose also with him. And by virtue of that communion which we had with him in all those actions of his, it is, that now when we are born again, we do all rise both from the guilt of sin and from the power of it: even as by virtue of the like communion we had with (or being one in) Adam, we come to be made sinful, when we begin first to exist as men, and to be first born.

Thus in his death he was considered as a common person, and God reckoned us dying then, and would have us reckon so also. So, Rom. 6:10, the apostle, speaking of Christ, saith, 'In that he died, he died unto sin once; but in that he liveth, he liveth unto God.' Then, verse 11, speaking of us, he says,

'Likewise reckon you yourselves to be dead unto sin, but alive unto God through Jesus Christ our Lord.' The meaning whereof is plainly this, that whereas regenerate men are for the present in the reality but imperfectly mortified and dead to sin, as considered in themselves, and in respect of the work of it, as wrought in them; yet that being considered in Christ as their head, and a common person representing them, they may λογιζειν [*logizein*], they may truly, by a way of faith, reason or 'reckon' themselves wholly dead, in and through Jesus Christ our Lord, in that once he died perfectly unto sin, as a common person representing them. So as what yet is wanting in the work of mortification, in their sense and experience of it, they may supply by faith, from the consideration of Christ their head, even themselves to have died when he died. The apostle, I say, would have them by reason conclude or infer (for so the word λογίζεσθε [*logizesthe*] signifies, as chapter 3:28, 'Therefore we conclude', *etc.*, it is the same word) from Christ's death, that they are dead; which conclusion cannot be made unless this be one of the propositions in this argument, that we died in Christ when he died; and so though in ourselves we are not yet wholly 'dead to sin', nor perfectly 'alive to God', yet 'through Jesus Christ your Lord and Head' (says he), 'reckon yourselves so', 'in that (as verse 10) he died and now lives', and you were included in him. And, indeed, this consideration the apostle suggests unto our faith, both as the greatest encouragement against imperfect mortification begun; that yet we may comfort ourselves by faith, as reckoning ourselves wholly dead in Christ's death, and so may assure ourselves we shall one day be perfectly dead in ourselves by virtue of it; and withal, as the strongest argument also and motive unto mortification, to endeavour to attain to the highest degree of it; which, therefore, he carries along in his discourse throughout that whole chapter. He would have them by faith or spiritual reasoning take in, and apprehend themselves long since dead to sin in Christ, when he died; and so should think it the greatest absurdity in the world to sin, even the least sin, we being dead long since, and that wholly, when Christ our head died: verse 2, 'and how shall we, that are dead to sin, live any longer therein?' and, verse 7, 'he that is dead is free from sin'; and how then shall we do the least service to it? Now all this he puts upon Christ's dying, and our dying then with him: verse 6, 'Knowing this, that our old man is crucified with him', even when he was crucified, 'that it might be destroyed' one day in us, fully and perfectly; Christ's body representing therein, as a public person, the elect, and their body of sin conjunct with them. So as thus by faith they are to reason themselves wholly dead to sin in Christ, and to use it as a reason and motive to stir up themselves not to yield to the least sin. I use this expression of being *wholly* dead, because if he had spoken merely of that *imperfect* mortification begun in us, the argument would not have been a perfect motive against the least sins. 'We who are dead, how shall we live in sin', or yield unto the least sin? For it might be said, alas! we are but imperfectly dead; and from an imperfect death could but an imperfect argument have been drawn. But the Scripture elsewhere tells us, that 'Christ by his death hath *perfected* for ever all that are sanctified'; so Heb. 10:14; so as in his death they may reckon themselves perfectly dead by faith, and perfectly sanctified, though yet the work be not actually and fully perfected.

And all this communion with Christ as a common person, representing them in his death, he there instructs them to be represented and sealed up to them by their baptism; so verses 3, 4. How, I shall show afterwards.

(4.) Now as this place holds forth Christ as a common person in his death representing us, so other places hold forth the like of his resurrection. In

1 Cor. 15:20, the apostle argues, that elect believers must and shall rise, because 'now Christ is risen from the dead, and is become the first-fruits of them that sleep'. See the force of this argument founded upon this notion and consideration, that Christ was a common person representing all the rest; and this strongly presented in that expression of his being 'the first-fruits', in allusion to the rite in the Levitical law. All the sheaves in a field being unholy of themselves, there was some one sheaf in the name and room of all the rest (which was called the first-fruit), which was lift up, and waved before the Lord; and so all the sheaves abroad in the field, by that act done to this one sheaf, were consecrated unto God, Lev. 23:10, *etc.*, by virtue of that law. The meaning of which rite, the apostle expounding, allegeth, Rom. 11:16, 'If the first-fruits be holy, all the lump is holy also.' Thus, when we were all dead, Christ as the first-fruits riseth, and this in our name and stead, and so we all rise with him and in him. And although the saints departed are not, in their own persons, as yet risen (as we all who are now alive are not in our own persons yet dead), yet, in the mean time, because thus they are risen in Christ, as their first-fruits, hence, in the very words following, he saith, they are but asleep, 'He is become the first-fruits of them that sleep', because they

remain alive in Christ their head, and shall rise one day, because in him they virtually are already risen; and this in God's account in as true and just a sense as we, though personally alive, are yet all reckoned dead in Adam, because he, as a common person, had the sentence of death pronounced on him, by virtue of which we must die; and this by the force of the same law, even of that which we have inculcated, of being a common person representing us. And indeed, so it follows (which argues this to be the apostle's meaning), verse 22, 'For as in Adam all die, even so in Christ shall all be made alive.' His argument lies thus: Adam was the first-fruits of them that died; Christ, of them that rise. Hence, therefore, we are elsewhere said (though in respect to another life) to be 'risen with Christ', Eph. 2:5, 6, and, which is yet more, 'to sit together with him in heaven'; because he, as a common person representing us, sits there in our name and stead, as you shall hear when I come to it in the text in the next section.

[Sect. 3]

Chapter 5

The second branch: How Christ's representing us as a common person in his resurrection, hath an influence into our justification, made forth by two things: (1.) How Christ at his resurrection was justified from our sin; (2.) That we were all then justified in him as a common person.

2. Now, then, to come to the other branch of the demonstration, namely, how this relation to us as a common person representing us in his resurrection, hath a real influence into our justification. And this is the point I drive at; and for the clearing of which that large and general discourse by way of digression in the former chapter was but to make way for.

I shall absolve and despatch this branch by showing two things:

(1.) That Christ himself was justified, and that at his resurrection.

(2.) That he was justified then as a common person, representing us therein, as well as that he rose as a common person; and so that we were then justified in him and with him; and by this means it is that by that act then done to him, our justification is made irrepealable for ever.

(1.) For the explicating of the first: As Christ was in his death made sin for us, and so sustained our persons in his satisfying for sin by his death (which is the matter of our righteousness), so in and upon his resurrection he was justified and acquitted from our sins by God, as having now fully in his death satisfied for them, which I make forth by these three things put together:

[1.] First, in reason, if that Christ were made sin for us, and satisfied for it, there must then some act pass, whereby Christ should be pronounced acquit of our sins, and fully clear of them, and so be himself formally justified in respect of those sins, for which he undertook to satisfy. For, according to the course of all proceedings, if a charge of guilt be formally laid, there must be as formal an act of acquitting, and of giving a *quietus est*.[1] There is no man but for his own discharge and security would desire it; nor is there any wise man that pays a debt for which he is legally sued, that will not have, upon the payment of it, as legal an acquittance. Paul, when he was cast into prison by a public act of authority, he stood upon it to have a public act of release from the same magistrates, and would not go forth of prison privily,

---

[1] Lit. 'he is quit'. The Latin phrase was originally used as a form of receipt or discharge on payment of a debt. — P.

though themselves sent to him so to go out, Acts 16:37. Now God himself did 'lay the iniquities of us all' upon Christ, Isa. 53:6, and 'had him to prison and judgment' for them, verse 8. There must, therefore, some act pass from God, legally to take them off from him, and declaring him discharged, to deliver him from prison and judgment.

And, *de facto*, it is evident that there was some such act passed from God; for, as we read, that Christ, while he lived, and also in his death, 'was made sin', and 'did bear the sin of many', as the phrase is, Heb. 9:28. So we read in the very next words, that 'he shall appear the second time *without sin*', which must needs be spoken in a direct opposition to his having borne our sins, and appearing then with all our sins laid to his charge. He appeared charged with them then, but now he shall appear, as apparently and manifestly to be without those sins, for of our sins it must needs be meant, and so to be discharged of them as fully as ever he appeared charged with them. For it is said, 'he shall *appear* without sin'; and therefore to the judgments of all it shall be made manifest, that that God that once charged him with them, hath now fully discharged him of them. The apostle speaks of it as of a great alteration made in this respect between Christ whilst on earth, and Christ as he is to appear the second time, and is now in heaven. And this alteration or discharge must necessarily be made by God; for he is the creditor who followed the suit, and therefore he alone can give the acquittance.

[2.] Now, secondly, from hence it will follow, that there must be some time when this alteration was first made, and discharge given, when Christ, from being sin, as he was made, should become without sin, through God's acquitting of him; and this, say I, was at his resurrection. It is not deferred as then to be first done, when he is to appear the second time, though then it *appears* indeed, but it is really done before; for he comes then to judge others for sin. Now in reason when should this acquittance or justification from our sins be first given to Christ, and legally pronounced on him, but when he had paid the last farthing of the debt, and made his satisfaction complete? which was then done when he began to rise; for his lying in the grave was a part of his humiliation, and so of his satisfaction, as generally orthodox divines hold. Now, therefore, when he began to rise, then ended his humiliation; and that was the first moment of his exaltation. His acquittance, therefore, bears date from thence, even from that very hour.

[3.] Hence, thirdly, we read, as that Christ was 'condemned', so that he was 'justified'. Thus, 1 Tim.

3:16, God is said to be 'manifest in the flesh', and
then that this God-man was 'justified in the Spirit'.
That is, whereas God was manifest or appeared in
flesh to condemn sin in the flesh, as Rom. 8, that same
God-man was also justified in the Spirit from all those
sins, and so 'received up to glory', as it follows there.
And not to go far, the very words of this my text, 'it is
God that justifies', are taken out of Isa. 50:8, 9, and
as there they are first spoken by Christ of himself,
then, when he 'gave his back to the smiters', in his
death (as in the verses before), and was put to death
as a 'condemned' man, he comforts himself with this,
'He is near that justifies me; who shall condemn?'
And when was that done, or to be done, but at his
resurrection? So the phrase in Timothy imports, if
you compare it with another in Peter, 1 Pet. 3:18.
'Being put to death in the flesh, and quickened in
[or by] the Spirit.' Paul, he says, 'justified in the
Spirit'; Peter, he says, 'quickened in the Spirit': both
mean one and the same thing. By *Spirit* is meant the
power of his Godhead and divine nature, whereby
he was at once both raised from the grave, and from
under the guilt of sin together. He was at once both
quickened, or raised, and justified also. And that by
Spirit they mean his divine nature, the opposition
in both places evidently implies; for it is opposed

to his *flesh*, or human nature. Now, because he was quickened, or raised, by the power of the Godhead, and at that raising him he was justified also by God, and declared justified by that resurrection, as he had been declared condemned by his death; hence, to *be justified* is put for his resurrection; for that was his justification, to declaration of all the world, that he was justified from all the sins laid to his charge. And that other place I cited out of Isaiah hath the same meaning also; for Christ there comforts himself against the Jews condemning him, and putting him to death, with the hopes of God's justifying of him, when he should have gone through that work. And Christ's meaning there is this, 'God will raise me up and acquit me', though you condemn and kill me. In the other prophets you shall find Christ still comforting himself against his condemnation at his death, with the thoughts of his resurrection, which he foresaw as shortly to follow after it; as here, in Isaiah, he comforts himself with these hopes of his being justified after their condemnation of him. For instance, Psa. 16:9, 'My flesh shall rest in hope: thou wilt not leave my soul in hell, nor suffer thy Holy One to see corruption.' Which words, you know, Peter, in the Acts, doth twice interpret of Christ's resurrection. In like manner here, in Isaiah, against his death and condemnation, he comforts himself with the hopes of God's justification of him at his resurrection, 'He is near who justifies me [and he shall help me]; who shall condemn?'

And further, to confirm and strengthen this notion, because his resurrection was the first moment of this his justification from our sins, therefore it is that God calls it his first begetting of Christ, 'This day have I begotten thee', speaking manifestly of his resurrection, Acts 13:33. And the reason of his so calling it, is, because all the while before he was covered with sin, and 'the likeness of sinful flesh'; but now, having flung it off, he appears like God's Son indeed, as if newly begotten. And thus also there cometh to be the fuller conformity between Christ's justification and ours. For as our justification is at our first being born again, so was Christ's also at this his first glorious begetting. He was under an attainder before; here was the act of restitution first passed. And as at our conversion (which is to us a resurrection) we 'pass from death to life', that is, from an estate of death and condemnation, unto justification of life, so did Christ also at his resurrection, which to him was a re-begetting, pass from an estate of death and guilt laid on him, to an estate of life and glory, and justification from guilt; and so shall 'appear', as the word is, Heb. 9:28 (as he doth now in heaven), 'without sin'; for he became to be without sin from that very moment. Thus I have shown how Christ was justified at his resurrection.

(2.) Now then, in the second place, I am to show that this his justification, and pronouncing him without sin, thus done at his resurrection, was done to him as the 'first-fruits', and as to a common person bearing our persons, and so in our names. From whence will necessarily follow, as the conclusion of all, that the persons of all the elect believers have been justified before God in Christ, as their head, at or from the time of his resurrection; and so that act of justification to have been so firmly passed as it cannot be revoked for ever. Now this is proved,

First, by the very same reason or respect that he was said to be the 'first-fruits of them that sleep', as representing the rest in his resurrection, which I showed at large in the former chapter; upon the same ground he is to be so looked at also in this his justification pronounced upon him at his resurrection, even as the first-fruits also of them that are justified. And so in the same sense, and by the same reason that we are said to be 'risen with Christ', in his resurrection; we must also be said to be 'justified with him', in this his justification, at his resurrection.

[Sect. 3]

And indeed (to enlarge this a little), as there is the same reason and ground for the one that there is for the other, he being a public person in both, so the rule will hold in all other things which God ever doth to us, or for us, which are common with Christ, and were done to him; that in them all Christ was the first-fruits, and they may be said to have been done in us, or to us, yea, by us, in him, and with him. Yea, whatever God meant to do for us and in us, whatever privilege or benefit he meant to bestow upon us, he did that thing first to Christ, and (some say) bestowed the like on him as a common person, that so it might be by a solemn formal act ratified, and be made sure to be done to us in our persons in due time, having first been done to him representing our persons; and that by this course taken, it might (when done to us) be effected by virtue of what was first done to him. Thus God meaning to sanctify us, he sanctifies Christ first, in him as a common person sanctifying us all; 'For their sakes I sanctify myself, that they also may be sanctified through thy truth', John 17:19. He sanctifies the human nature of Christ personal (that is his body), and him first, as a common person representing us, that so we, being virtually and representatively sanctified in him, may be sure to be sanctified afterwards in our own persons, by means of his sanctification. And so in like manner for our sakes he was 'justified in the Spirit'; because we were to be justified, and so to be justified first in him, and with him as a common person. Now this rule holds in all blessings else bestowed; for Paul pronounceth of them all, that 'God hath blessed us with all spiritual blessings in Christ Jesus', Eph. 1:3, which God did so order, that, as he speaks of ordaining salvation to be by faith, Rom. 4:16, that all those 'blessings might be sure to all the seed'. For this formal investiture of estating us into all blessings by such solemn acts done to Christ as our head and representer of us, makes what he intends to bestow sure beforehand, by an irrepealable act and sentence, which hath its warrant in all laws of men, as I have shown, and shall anon again urge. And,

Secondly, by the equity of the same law that in Adam we were all condemned, Adam being a type of him in this, by the same law, I say, we were all justified in Christ when he was justified, else the type were not therein fulfilled. Now the sentence of condemnation was first passed upon Adam alone, yet considered as a common person for us; therefore also this acquittance and justification was then passed towards Christ alone, as a public person for us. Yea, in this his being justified, Christ must much rather be considered as a common person representing us, than Adam was in his condemnation. For Christ in his own person, as he had no sin, so he had no need of any justification from sin, nor should ever have been condemned. And therefore this must be only in a respect unto our sins imputed to him; and if so, then in our stead. And so herein, he was more purely to be considered as a common person for us, than ever Adam was, in his being condemned. For Adam, besides his standing as a common person for us, was furthermore condemned in his own person; but Christ in being justified from sin, could only be considered as standing for others. Thus, Rom. 5:18, 'Therefore as by the offence of one, judgment came upon all men to condemnation; even so [or in like manner] by the righteousness of that one man Christ, the free gift came upon all men [namely, in Christ] unto justification of life.' He parallels both with a *so*, only with this difference between Adam's being a common person for us, and so between the ground of our being condemned in him, and Christ his being a common person for us, and our acquittance in him, that the 'condemnation came upon all' by a necessary, natural covenant, for by such a covenant was Adam appointed a common person for us; but Christ his being appointed thus a common person for us, it was by a 'free gift' of grace; and therefore in like manner by a free gift of grace it is that the imputation of that which he did, or was done to him, is reckoned ours. As then 'in Adam all died', when he sinned, as the apostle speaks, so in Christ 'were all justified', when he was justified. For as in his death Christ was a public person for us, and in all that befell him; so in his resurrection, and in all that was then done to him; and so, in this his being then justified. And as when he died, 'the just was put to death for the unjust' (as Peter speaks), so when he arose and was justified, the just that needed no justification was justified for the unjust, who else had been condemned; and so we were then justified with him.

Chapter 6

How our faith may raise from hence just matter of triumph about our justification.—An explication how we are justified by faith, although justified in Christ at his resurrection.

And hereupon is grounded this triumph of faith here, from Christ's resurrection, 'Who shall condemn? It is Christ that is risen.' The meaning whereof is, that he was justified at his resurrection (*justified in the Spirit* and *quickened in the Spirit* being all one), and 'we in him'. Yea, and a *rather* is put upon this, rather than put upon his death; for this act was a solemn discharge from all sin and condemnation; it was a legal acquittance given to Christ for all our sins, and so to us also considered as in him. His death was but the satisfaction and payment; but this is the first act of absolution. Yea, and this is the original act, which is upon record between God and Christ; and our justification and atonement (when we are justified by faith in Christ) is but a copy fetched from this roll, and court-sentence then pronounced.

And such a way and course to ratify and make acts good and legal, even to have them done by another representing one's person, is common among men, as those instances I formerly gave do show. An attorney-at-law receives a debt, or an acquittance for a debt, paid or given for another man, and it is as legal as if the man himself or creditor had done it, and the debtor had received the acquittance himself. Yea, acts of the greatest and highest concernment are ofttimes no otherwise transacted; as the marriages of princes are by proxy solemnized, their ambassadors representing their persons, and contracting and marrying their wives in their stead, which acts are thereby made as irrevocable, and irrepealable, as if themselves had in person done them. And so if we were justified when Christ did rise and was justified, our justification then cannot be reversed, but stands as legal and warrantable as any act that God or man ever ratified or confirmed. And 'who shall condemn?'

Only, for farther explication's sake, lest there be a mistake, let me add this, that it is necessary that we be justified in our own persons by faith (notwithstanding this former act thus legally passed), whereby we lay hold upon what God did thus before for us in Christ, to the end that God upon our believing may, according to his own rules, justify his justifying of us unto all the world; which, until we do believe, he could not do. For according to the revealed rules of his word, which he professeth to proceed by at the latter day, there is a curse and a sentence of condemnation pronounced against us, under which we stand till he shall take it off by giving us faith; unto which he hath, in the same word, made the promise of justifying us in our own persons, as before he had done in Christ. Yet still notwithstanding, so as although, when we first believe, then only justification is actually and personally applied to us, yet at Christ's resurrection, and in his being then justified, this act and sentence was virtually pronounced upon us; and so doth necessarily require, and exact at God's hands, the bestowing faith upon us; that so by virtue of this former act passed, we come to be actually justified in our own consciences, and before all the world. And so our justification, which was but secretly wrought and passed upon us in Christ, is never made void, but stands irrepealable; and so ratified, that our personal justification by faith doth always infallibly second and succeed it. And (to illustrate it a little) our condemnation in Adam, and this our justification in Christ, do in this hold parallel together, that as in Adam we were all virtually condemned, 'in Adam all die',—and that legal enough too, for thereupon came out that statute-law, *statutum est*,[1] 'It is appointed' that all should die, and yet we are not actually in our own persons condemned till we are born of him; nor do we personally die, until we lay down our flesh,—even so it is in the matter of our justification: it was done virtually in Christ, and afterwards, when we believe, is actually passed in and upon ourselves. Now I call this former but a virtual justification, even as by the sentence of condemnation passed upon a malefactor, he is called a dead man, that is, he is so virtually and in law (as we say), though naturally he die not many

---

[1] Latin: it is established.—P.

days after, but in that respect may be still alive; so by Christ's being justified, we are all virtually and in law justified, through a secret irrepealable covenant between God and Christ, who only did then 'know who were his'.

And for a confirmation even of this also, that God accounts all the elect justified in his justifying of Christ, we shall not need to go any further than the words of this text, if we do but diligently compare their standing here with that of theirs in that place out of which they are taken, and where we find them first recorded and spoken, namely, in that 50th of Isaiah, verses 7, 8, 'He is near that justifies me; who is he that shall condemn?' Now there (as interpreters agree, and as the context shows), those words are spoken by Christ himself; for, verse 5, he speaks of God's 'boring his ear' to do his will (the same expression that is used of Christ, Psa. 40:6), and farther says, 'I gave my back to the smiters, and my cheeks to them that pulled off the hair, and I hid not my face from shame and spitting' (all which you may read in Christ's sufferings, Matt. 26:67 and 27:26). And he spake before (in verse 4), of God's having 'given him the tongue of the learned, to speak a word in season to him that is weary', which you may read done by Christ, Matt. 11:28. Now those

words were spoken by Christ, to comfort himself
against the Jews condemning him, as considering that
God would justify him; as at his resurrection, you
have heard, he did. Now mark it, those very words
which Isaiah brings in Christ speaking as of himself
alone, those very words Paul here boldly applies,
in the like triumph, to all the elect of Christ, 'Who
shall condemn? It is God that justifies'; and this
because Christ is dead, and risen, and acquitted by
God. Christ spake those words as a public person in
the name of all his elect, whom he in his death and
in his justification represented; and for that very
respect Paul speaks the like words over again, of all
elect believers, as being as truly and really intended
of them, when spoken by Christ, as of himself, and
of his own person. 'He is near that justifies me [says
Christ]; who shall condemn?' namely, me, or mine
elect, whose persons I sustain. And 'Who shall lay
anything to the charge of God's elect?' says Paul. 'It
is God that justifies; who shall condemn?' for Christ
hath died, and been condemned for them, and Christ
was justified from that condemnation, and they in
him. And because the justification of himself, which
Christ spake of, as looked for from God, was to be
made at his resurrection, as hath been said, therefore
Paul here puts a *rather* upon his resurrection.

And farther to establish this, as you heard before out of Rom. 6:11, that in respect of sanctification we were dead with Christ, even then when he died; so in Col. 2:13, we are said to be 'risen with him', in respect of our justification, which is the thing in hand. The words are, 'And you being dead in your sins', namely, the guilt of your sins, 'and the circumcision of your flesh', that is, in respect of the power of corrupt nature, 'hath he quickened together with him, *having forgiven you all your trespasses.*' See here, the forgiveness of our sins, or our justification, is called a 'quickening' or 'a raising up of us' (as the 12th verse hath it), 'together with him', in a conformity and relation to that justification from our sins, which at his resurrection he received in our names. His meaning is, he was justified then, and in our names; and so we are now justified through the virtue of that our communion with him therein. For if you mark the connection of the words with what follows, verse 14, you will find this 'forgiving of their trespasses [verse 13] through their being quickened together with him', not only to have been done when they believed, and so when they had that justification personally first applied to them, of which, it is true, the words in the 12th verse are to be understood, but also then to have been done, 'when he having [as it follows in the 14th verse] blotted out the handwriting of ordinances which was against us, nailing it to his cross, and having spoiled principalities and powers', and got the victory, namely, in his rising again, 'had made a show of them openly' (in his ascending to heaven), 'triumphing over them ἐν αὐτῷ [*en auto*] in himself' (as the margin hath it);[1] of which words I shall farther speak in the next head. So as then when Christ did this in himself, then were our sins forgiven, then were we acquitted with him, and triumphed with him, he doing all this in our stead, representing us.

Chapter 7

*How all this, both the support of our faith and our justif-
ication by Christ's resurrection, is sealed up to us in
baptism.—The conclusion.—How faith may make use
of Christ's resurrection in its pleas to God.*

And all this our communion with Christ in his resurrection, both in respect of sanctification, which the 6th of the Romans holds forth, and of justification, which this place in the Colossians holds forth, is lively (as both places declare) set out, and sealed up to us, in the sacrament of baptism. Romans 6:3, 4,

[1] A reference to the marginal notes of the AV (1611).—P.

we are said to be 'buried with him in baptism', *etc.*; and Colossians 2:12, 'buried with him in baptism, wherein also you are risen with him'. The eminent thing signified and represented in baptism is not simply the blood of Christ as it washeth us from sin; but there is a farther representation therein of Christ's death, burial, and resurrection, in the baptized's being first buried under water, and then rising out of it; and this not in a bare conformity unto Christ, but in a representation of a communion with Christ in that, his death and resurrection. Therefore it is said, 'we are buried with him in baptism'; and 'wherein you are risen with him'. It is not simply said, *like as* he was buried, and rose, but *with him*. So as our communion and oneness with him in his resurrection, is represented to us therein, and not only our conformity or likeness unto him therein. And so baptism representeth this to us, that Christ having once in himself sustained the persons of all the elect, in his burial and resurrection, that now, upon the party himself who is baptized, is personally, particularly, and apparently re-acted the same part again, in his baptism; thereby showing what his communion with Christ before was, in what was then done to Christ; that he then was buried with Christ, and rose with him; and upon that ground is now in this outward sign of baptism, as in a show or representation, both buried and also riseth again.

And moreover, hence it is, that the 'answer of a good conscience', which is made the inward effect of this ordinance of baptism, 1 Pet. 3:21, is there also attributed unto Christ's resurrection, as the thing signified and represented in baptism, and as the cause of that answer of a good conscience. 'Even baptism', saith he, 'doth now also save us', as being the ordinance that seals up salvation, 'not the putting away of the filth of the flesh', or the washing of the outward man; 'but the answer of a good conscience towards God, *by the resurrection of Jesus Christ.*' To open these words: Our consciences are that principle in us which are the seat of the guilt of all the sins of the whole man; unto whose court they all come to accuse us, as unto God's deputy; which conscience is called good or evil, as the state of the man is. If his sin remain unpardoned, then as his estate is damnable, so his conscience is evil. If his sins be forgiven, and his person justified, his conscience is said to be good; conscience having its denomination from the man's state, even as the urine is called good or bad, as the state of the man's body is healthful or unsound whose urine it is. Now in baptism, forgiveness of sins and justification being sealed up to a believer's faith and conscience, under that lively representation of his communion with Christ in his resurrection; hence this is made the fruit of baptism, that the good conscience of a believer, sealed up in baptism, hath wherewithal from thence to answer all accusations of sin that can or do at any time come in upon him; and all this, as it is here added, 'by virtue of the resurrection of Jesus Christ'; namely, in this respect, that his communion with Christ in his resurrection hath been represented in his baptism as a ground of his faith, and of that 'answer' unto all accusations. So that indeed the same thing that Paul says by way of triumph and defiance to all accusations, 'Who shall condemn? Christ is risen'; the very same thing Peter here mentions, though not by way of defiance, yet of a believer's answer and apology, that if sins do come to condemn or accuse, a good conscience is ready to say, 'Christ is risen', and I was then 'justified in him'. There is my answer, which nothing in heaven or hell is able to reply unto. 'This is the answer of a good conscience, by the resurrection of Jesus Christ.'

Now to crown this second pillar of faith with this *coronis* or conclusion, by way of application or direction to a believer's faith, how to make use of Christ's resurrection in point of non-condemnation. You heard before, out of Romans 6, that in respect of mortification (as the apostle there reasoneth) we may be truly said to have been 'perfectly dead to all sin' in Christ's 'dying unto sin once'; and through his representing us therein as dying unto sin, in and with him. So as although we be for the present but imperfectly mortified in ourselves, yet when corruptions arise, the apostle bids us help ourselves against them by faith, 'reasoning' ourselves to stand wholly dead to sin, when Christ died; and so to conclude from thence, that we shall one day be fully dead to sin, because we then did perfectly die in Christ unto it; which kind of reasoning also God would have us use as a motive (and of all motives that are in the gospel it is the strongest) against any corruption whenas it ariseth. 'Shall I that am dead to sin' in Christ, and so am freed from it, 'shall I live any longer therein?' verse 2. Now as God would have our faith make this use of our communion with Christ in his death, in point of sanctification, just so, when guilt of sin ariseth in thy conscience to accuse or threaten condemnation, reason thou thyself (as the apostle's word in that other case), or 'reckon thyself' (as our translation hath it) justified in Christ, in his justification, which was done at his resurrection. Yea, and seeing God would have thee use thy communion with Christ in his death, as an argument to move thee to mortify sin, bidding thee to reckon thyself dead to sin in Christ, do thou desire him, in like manner, to reckon thee as justified at Christ's resurrection (for the ground of both is the same), and return that as an argument to him to move him to justify thee. And this is that answer of a good conscience which Peter speaks of; this is the meaning of Paul's challenge, 'Who shall condemn? Christ is risen.' And should thy heart object and say, But I know not whether I was one of those that God reckoned justified with Christ when he arose; then go thou to God, and ask him boldly, whether he did not do this for thee, and whether thou wert not one of them intended by him. Put God to it, and God will (by virtue of Christ's resurrection for thee) even himself answer thy faith this question ere thou art aware. He will not deny it. And to secure thee the more, know that however Christ will be sure to look to that for thee; so as that thou having been then intended, — as, if thy heart be drawn to give itself up to Christ, thou wert, — shalt never be condemned.

SECTION 4

FAITH SUPPORTED BY CHRIST'S ASCENSION, AND SITTING AT GOD'S RIGHT HAND

Who is he that condemneth? It is Christ, ... who is even at the right hand of God.
ROM. 8:34.

Chapter 1

*A connection of this third head with the two former; show-
ing how it affords a farther degree of triumph. — Two
things involved in it: 1. Christ's ascension; 2. Christ's
power and authority in heaven.*

I come next to this third great pillar and support
of faith, Christ's being at God's right hand; and to
show how the view and consideration hereof may
strengthen faith seeking justification and pardon of
sin; 'Who is he that condemneth? Christ is even at
God's right hand.'

In the opening of which, I shall keep to the begun
method, both by showing how justification itself
depends upon this, and the *evidence* thereof to us;
both which the apostle had here in his eye, and from
both which our faith may derive comfort and assurance. And I mean to keep punctually to the matter
of justification only, as in the former.

These two latter that remain here in the text —
Christ sitting at God's right hand, and his interceding
for us — are brought in here by the apostle, as those

which have a redundant force and prevalency in them, for the non-condemnation of the elect; that although the two former abundantly served to secure it, yet these two added to the former, do make the triumph of faith more complete and full, and us 'more than conquerors', as it after follows. Nor doth this place alone make mention of Christ's 'sitting at God's right hand', which I now am first to handle, in this its relation, and influence into our justification, and the assurance of faith about it; but you have it to the same end, use, and purpose, alleged by that other great apostle, 1 Pet. 3:18-22. And if the scopes of these two apostles in both places be compared, they are the same. Here the resurrection of Christ, and his sitting at God's right hand, are brought in as the ground of this bold challenge and triumph of faith; and there, in Peter, is mentioned the answer or plea of a good conscience in a believer justified, which it puts into the court, and opposeth against all condemning guilts (so it is called, verse 21), the apostle alleging the resurrection of Jesus Christ as one ground of it, 'the answer of a good conscience, by the resurrection of Jesus Christ'. And then further to back and strengthen this plea or answer of a good conscience, the apostle puts his ascension and sitting at God's right hand into the bill, as further grounds confirming it; so it follows, 'who is gone to heaven, and is at the right hand of God, angels, and authorities, and powers, being made subject to him'. All which the apostle here expresseth in one word (as enough to carry it) that Christ is 'even at God's right hand'. The soul hath sufficient answer against condemnation in Christ's death and resurrection, full enough though it should stop there; yea therein can faith triumph, though it went no further; for it can show a full satisfaction given in his death, and that accepted by God for us, and Christ acquitted, and we in him. Therefore, faith (you see) comes to a *rather* there. But then, let it go on, to consider Jesus sitting at God's right hand, and making intercession for us; and then faith will triumph and insult over all accusers, be more than a conqueror; then it comes not to a *rather* only, as here, but to a *'much more shall we be saved by his life'*, thus Rom. 5:10. And the meaning thereof is, that if his death had power to pay all our debts, and justify us at first, then much more hath his life this power. So that his death is but the ground and foundation of our faith herein, and the lowest step of this ladder, but these other are the top and full triumph of faith therein. And our spirits should rise, as the apostle here riseth. Faith upon these wings may not only fly above the gunshot of all accusations and condemners, but even clean out of their sight, and so far above all such thoughts and fears, as it may reach to a security that sins are forgotten and shall be remembered no more. What joy was there in the disciples, when they saw Christ risen! John 20. Therefore in the primitive times it was used as a voice of joy; and to this day the Grecian Christians so entertain each other, at that time of the year, with these words, 'The Lord is risen', your Surety is out of prison, fear not. But (as Christ said in another case, so say I) what will you say, if you see your Surety ascended up to heaven, and that, as far 'above angels and principalities' (as the apostle speaks, Eph. 1) as the heavens are above the earth? Will you not in your faiths and hopes proportionably ascend, and climb up also, and have thoughts of pardon, as far exceeding your ordinary thoughts as the heavens are above the earth? Therefore, first view him as ascending into heaven, ere ever he comes to be at God's right hand, and see what matter of triumph that will afford you; for that you must first suppose, ere you can see him at God's right hand, and so is necessarily included, though not expressed here. But that place fore-quoted out of Peter (1 Pet. 3:18-22) gives us both these two particulars included in it: 1. His ascension (who is gone into heaven); and

2. his power and authority there (is at God's right hand, and hath all power and authority subject to him), and prompts both these, as fit matter to be put into a good conscience, its answer and apology why it should not be condemned; and therefore both may here as well come in into faith's triumph, and that as being intended also by the apostle, and included in this one expression. He speaks with the least, to show what cause faith had to triumph, for the least expression of it; his purpose being but to give a hint of faith, or that which comprehensively contains many things in it, which he would have us distinctly to consider for our comfort.

Chapter 2

Showing first what evidence for our justification Christ's ascension into heaven affords unto our faith, upon that first forementioned consideration of his being a Surety for us.

1. First, then, to see what triumph his ascending into heaven will add unto our faith in matter of non-condemnation.

(1.) And herein, first, there is not nothing[1] in it to consider what he then did, and what was his last act when he was to take his rise, to fly up to heaven. He 'blessed his disciples', and thereby left a blessing upon earth with them, for all his elect, to the end of the world. The true reason and mind of which blessing them was, that he being now to go to execute the eternal office of his priesthood in heaven (of which God had sworn, 'Thou art a priest for ever after the order of Melchisedec'); as Melchisedec in the type blessed Abraham, and in him all the faithful as in his loins,—therefore the apostle said that 'Levi paid tithes unto Melchisedec in Abraham's loins', therefore he was blessed in his loins,—so did Christ begin this new and second part of his priesthood with blessing the apostles, and in them all the elect to the end of the world. This was the last thing that Christ did on earth, yea this he did whilst ascending, 'he was taken up whilst he did it'. So Luke 24:50, 51. And thus solemnly he now did this, to show that the curse was gone, and that sin was gone, and that action speaks thus much, as if Christ himself had said it; O my brethren (for so he styled his disciples after his resurrection), I have been dead, and in dying made a curse for you; now that curse I have fully removed,

---

[1] That is, 'there is something', or 'it is not useless'.—Ed.

and my Father hath acquitted me and you for it; and now I can be bold to bless you, and pronounce all your sins forgiven, and your persons justified. For that is the intendment and foundation of blessing. 'Blessed is the man whose sins are forgiven him', and therefore that was the true meaning of his blessing them; which he reserved thus as his last act, to show how by his death he had redeemed them from the curse of the law, and now going to heaven, was able to bless them with all the spiritual blessings that are there, and which heaven can afford, for *heavenly* they are called in that respect, Eph. 1:3. And as in Abraham (blessed by Melchisedec) all the faithful were blessed, so, in these apostles, all the elect to come are blessed. As when God individually blessed Adam and Eve at the first creation, yet he in them, blessed all that were for ever to come of them; so Christ in blessing them, blessed us, and all 'that shall believe through their word', to the end of the world. And that they were thus then to be considered as common persons, receiving this blessing for us all, appeareth by Christ's words then uttered, 'I am with you to the end of the world' (*i.e.*, with you and all your successors, both ministers and other believers), Matt. 28:20. And Christ herein did as God did before him. When God had done his work of creation, he 'looked upon all he had done, and saw that it was good, and he blessed it'. Thus did Jesus Christ; now that he had by that 'one offering perfected for ever all the elect', he comfortably vieweth and pronounceth it perfect, and them blessed; and so goes to heaven, to keep and enjoy the Sabbath of all there.

(2.) Now, secondly, let us see him ascending, and see what comfort that will also afford our faith, towards the persuasion of justification. The apostles stood gazing on him; and so do you lift up your hearts to gaze on him by faith, and view him in that act, as he is passing along into heaven, as leading sin, hell, death, and devil in triumph, at his chariot wheels. And therewith let your faith triumph, in a further evidence of justification. Thus, Eph. 4:8, out of Psa. 68:18, the apostle saith, 'When he ascended up on high, he led captivity captive' (to which Hebraism the Latin phrase, *vincere victoriam*, to win a victory, doth answer): then he led captive all our spiritual enemies, that would have captived us, they being now captived. Now leading of captives is always after a perfect victory. And therefore, whereas at his death he had conquered them, at his rising scattered them, now at his ascension he leads them captive. And so that Psalm in the type begins, verse 1, 'Let God *arise*, and let his enemies *be scattered*, let them flee before him'; so at his resurrection they did. And then he ascends in triumph (as here) in token of victory, 'he is ascended up on high', verse 18. He ascends, as David after his victory, up to Mount Sion (for the celebrating of which that Psalm seems to have been made by David), whereof this was the intended type.

And two *actus triumphales*, triumphing acts there were, here mentioned:

[1.] Leading the captives bound to his chariot wheels; as the manner of the Roman triumph was, when the conqueror went up to the Capitol; and other heathens in David's time; as Achilles led Hector captive, who tied his feet to his chariot wheels, and dragged him dead round about the walls of Troy. Now thus did Christ then deal with our sins and all other enemies.

[2.] The second act is casting abroad of gifts, 'He gave gifts to men.' It was the custom at their triumphs to cast new coins (*missilia*) abroad among the multitude; so doth Christ throw the greatest gifts for the good of men, that ever were given. Therefore, 'who shall condemn?' Sins and devils are not only dead, but triumphed over. Compare with this that other place, Col. 2:15, 'Having spoiled principalities and powers, he made a show of them openly, triumphing over them in himself.' So I read it, and the Greek bears it, and so it is in the margin varied. It is a manifest allusion unto the manner of triumphs after victories among the Romans, even unto two of the most notable parts thereof: the first, of spoiling the enemy upon the place, ere they stirred out of the field; and this was done by Christ on the cross. 'Having spoiled them' first, as verse 15 hath it. He speaks it of the devils, our enemies and accusers; they had all God's threatenings in his law, and the ceremonial law (the bond for our debt unto the moral law) to show for it; in these lay the power of the devil over us, that he could boldly come to God and accuse us, and sue our bond. And therefore, Heb. 2:14, he is said to have 'the power of death'. Now Christ first took away all his power, and spoiled him of all his ensigns, weapons, and colours; which he did on the place where the battle was fought, namely, on the cross; and 'nailed our bond' thereto, and, having paid the debt, left the bond cancelled, ere he stirred off the cross. But then, having thus spoiled these enemies on the cross, he further makes a public triumphal show of them in his own person, which is a second act; as the manner of the Roman emperors was, in their great triumphs, to ride through the city in the greatest state, and have all the spoils carried before them, and the kings and nobles whom they

[Sect. 4]

had taken they tied to their chariots, and led them as captives. And this did Christ at his ascension (for of his triumphing at his ascension I take this triumph in this Epistle to the Colossians to be understood, and so to be interpreted by that fore-cited 4th of the Ephesians); he plainly manifesting by this public open show of them at his ascension, that he had spoiled and fully subdued them on the cross. That which hath diverted interpreters from thinking this of Col. 2 to have been the triumph of his ascension hath been this, that the triumph is said to have been made ἐν αὐτῷ, [*en auto*] which they interpret '*in it*', as if it referred to the cross (mentioned verse 14), as the place of it; whenas it may as well be translated '*in himself*', *i.e.*, 'in his own power and strength', noting how he alone did this, which other conquerors do not: they conquer not in themselves, and by themselves, which Christ did. And yet it was the law, that if the Roman emperors or generals themselves took anything in war, they had a peculiar honour to dedicate it in triumph more peculiarly. Now Christ conquered in himself, and therefore triumphed in himself, and himself alone. And thus it became our Redeemer (like another Samson) not only to break sin's bars, and fling off hell-gates, and come out of that prison he was in; but, as in sign of a trophy, to take them on his back, and carry them up the hill, as Samson (the type of him) did the gates of the city to an high hill, himself triumphantly carrying them on his own shoulders.

Now did Christ then, who was your Surety, thus triumph? Then let your faith triumph likewise; for this was not only done by your Surety, but in your stead; seeing this *for us* here is to be put to each thing mentioned. The apostle calls for this at our hands here. 'We are more than conquerors', says he, verse 37.

(3.) Then, thirdly, see him entering into heaven: when he comes first to court after this great undertaking, how doth God look on him? Is God satisfied with what he hath done? As, you know, when a general comes home, there useth to be great observing how the king takes his service, as performed according to commission. Christ as a Surety undertook for sinners fully to conquer all our enemies; and God bade him look that he did it perfectly, or never see his face more, Heb. 5:8, 9. He was to be 'perfect through sufferings', and those sufferings to be such as 'to perfect' us also Heb. 10:14. Now, behold, your Surety is like a conqueror entered heaven: let that convince you that he hath satisfied the debt, and performed his commission to a tittle. God would never have suffered him to come thither else; but as soon as ever his head had peeped into heaven, have sent him down again to perform the rest. But God lets him enter in, and he comes boldly and confidently, and God lets him stay there. Therefore be convinced that he hath given God full satisfaction. Christ himself useth this argument, as the strongest that could be brought to 'convince the world' that this righteousness (which he had in his doctrine taught them) was the righteousness which men were only to be saved by, the true righteousness of God indeed. John 16:8-10, He 'shall convince the world of righteousness'; that is, work faith in the hearts of men, to believe and lay hold on my righteousness, as the true righteousness that God hath ordained; and this 'because [says he] I go to my Father, and you shall see me no more'. That is, by this argument and evidence it is and shall be evinced, that I who undertook to satisfy for sin, and to procure a perfect righteousness, have perfectly performed it; and that it is a righteousness which God's justice doth accept of, to save sinners by; in that I, after my death, and finishing this work, will ascend up to my Father, into heaven, and keep my standing there, and you shall see me no more: whereas, if I had not fulfilled all righteousness, and perfectly satisfied God, you may be sure there would be no going to heaven for me, nor remaining there. God would send me down again, to do the rest, and you should certainly see me with shame sent back again; but 'I go to heaven, and you shall see me no more.'

Chapter 3

Showing what evidence also Christ's sitting at God's right hand, having been our Surety, affords to our faith for justification.

2. Now then, in the next place, for his being or sitting at God's right hand, which is the second particular to be spoken of. As soon as Christ was carried into heaven, look, as all the angels fell down and worshipped him, so his Father welcomed him, with the highest grace that ever yet was shown. The words which he then spake we have recorded, Psa. 110, 'Sit thou at my right hand, till I make thine enemies thy footstool.' You may by the way observe, for the illustration of this, how upon all the several parts of performance of his office, either God is brought in speaking to Christ, or Christ to his Father. Thus, when he chose him first to be our Mediator, he takes an oath, 'Thou art a priest for ever, after the order of Melchisedec.' Again, when Christ came to take upon him our nature,

[Sect. 4]

the words he spake are recorded, 'Lo, I come to do thy will, a body hast thou fitted me': so Heb. 10:5-7, out of the 40th Psalm. Likewise, when he hung upon the cross, his words unto God are recorded, Psa. 22:1, 'My God, my God, why hast thou forsaken me?' In like manner, when he rose again, God's words used then to him are recorded, 'Thou art my Son, this day have I begotten thee' Psa. 2, which place is expounded of the resurrection, Acts 13:33, which is as much as if he had said, Thou never appearedst like my Son till now; for whereas I chose a Son to be glorified with power and majesty, hitherto thou hast appeared only as 'a son of man' (*Enosh*, sorry man); hitherto thou hast been made sin, and a curse; not like my Son, but hast appeared 'in the likeness of sinful flesh', and of 'a servant', all besmeared with blood; therefore this is the first day wherein I make account 'I have begotten thee'; even now, when thou first beginnest to appear out of that sinful hue and likeness of sinful flesh: now I own thee for my Son indeed. And in him he owned us all thus at his resurrection. And then, last of all, when he comes into heaven, the first word God speaks to him is, Son, 'sit thou at my right hand'; thou hast done all my work, and now I will do thine; (he gives him a *Quietus est*) rest here; 'sit here, till I make all thy enemies thy footstool'.

And now, what say you, are ye satisfied yet, that God is satisfied for your sins? What superabundant evidence must this Christ's sitting at God's right hand give to a doubting heart? It argues, *first*, that Christ, for his part, hath perfectly done his work; and that there is no more left for him to do by way of satisfaction. This the word *sitting* implies. *Secondly*, it argues that God is as fully satisfied on his part: this his sitting *at God's right hand* implies.

(1.) For the *first*; the phrase of *sitting* doth betoken rest, when work is fulfilled and finished. Christ was not to return till he had accomplished his work, Heb. 10:11, 12. The apostle comparing the force and excellency of Christ's sacrifice, with those of the priests of the old law, says, that 'those priests *stood* daily offering of sacrifices, which can never take sins away'. Their *standing* implied that they could never make satisfaction, so as to say, 'we have finished it'. But Christ (says he, verse 12), 'after he had offered up one sacrifice for ever, *sat down*', *etc.* Mark how he opposeth their *standing* to his *sitting down*. He sat as one who had done his work. Thus, Heb. 4:10, 'he that is entered into his rest'—speaking of Christ, as I have elsewhere shown—'hath ceased from his work, as God from his'.

(2.) Secondly, this, his being *at God's right hand*,

as strongly argues that God is satisfied; for if God had not been infinitely well pleased with him, he would never have let him come so near him, much less have advanced him so high as his right hand. And, therefore, in that place even now cited (Heb. 10:10-12, compared with the former verses), this is alleged as an evidence that Christ had 'for ever taken sins away' (which those priests of the law could not do, who therefore 'often offered the same sacrifice', as verse 11). That 'this man, after he had offered one sacrifice for sins for ever, sat down on the right hand of God', as thereby showing (and that most manifestly) that he had at that once offered up such a satisfactory sacrifice as had pleased God for ever; and thereupon took up his place at God's right hand as an evidence of it; so possessing the highest place in court. This setting him at God's right hand, is a token of special and highest favour. So kings, whom they were most pleased with, they did set at their right hands, as Solomon did his mother, 1 Kings 2:19; and so Christ, the church his queen, Psa. 45:9, and it was a favour which God never after vouchsafed to any, Heb. 1:13, 'To which of all the angels did he say, Sit thou at my right hand?' Therefore, Phil. 2:9, it is not only said that he 'exalted him', but, *superexaltavit*, 'he highly exalted him', so as never any was exalted;

for he was 'made thereby higher than the heavens'. Thus much for the first head.

Chapter 4

Demonstrates, in the second place, what influence Christ's ascension hath in a believer's non-condemnation, upon that second premised consideration of Christ's being a common person for us. — The security that faith may have from thence.

We have thus seen what triumphing evidence and demonstration, both Christ's ascension and sitting at God's right hand, do afford us for this, that Christ being considered as our *Surety*, hath therefore undoubtedly subdued our enemies and sins, and satisfied God. Let us now consider further, what force, efficacy, and influence these two (both his ascending and sitting at God's right hand as an head and common person for us) have in them towards the assured working and accomplishment of the salvation of believers, his elect. And from the consideration of this, which is a second head, our faith may be yet further confirmed and strengthened in its confidence. 'Who shall condemn? It is Christ that is at God's right hand.'

I shall take in (as in the former) both his ascension and sitting at God's right hand.

1. And first for his *ascending*; consider these two things in it which may uphold our confidence.

(1.) That the great end and purpose of that his ascending, the errand, the business he ascended for, was 'to prepare and provide a place for us', and to make way for our coming thither. This he assures his disciples of, John 14:2, 'In my Father's house are many mansions: I go to prepare a place for you'; as Joseph was secretly sent before by God's intendment to prepare a place in Egypt for his brethren, whom God's providence meant to bring after him, so more openly doth Christ ascend to heaven, professedly declaring that to be his business: 'I go to prepare a place for you', and it is my Father's house, saith he, where I can provide for you and make you welcome. You heard before, what welcome God gave Christ when he first arrived there, and what he said to him, and Christ said (as it were) again to God: I come not alone, I have much company, many of my brethren and followers to come after (for it was the declared and avowed end of his coming to prepare a place for them), I prayed when I was on earth, 'that where I am they might be also', John 17:24; and now I am come hither, my train must come in too, I am not complete without them; if you receive me you must receive them also, and I am come to take up lodgings for them. Thus the Captain of our salvation, being 'made perfect through sufferings', and then 'crowned with glory and honour', in 'bringing of many sons to glory' as Heb. 2:9, 10, of which company he was Captain, is brought in saying to God, verse 13, 'Behold I and the children which God hath given me', he speaks it when brought to glory. I am their Captain, and they must follow me; where I am they must be. Lo! I am here, and am not to come alone, but to bring to glory all the children which thou hast given me. They shall be all welcome (says God), there is room enough for them, 'many mansions'; so that we need not fear, nor say in our hearts doubting and despairing, 'Who shall ascend up to heaven for us', to bring us thither? (as Rom. 10:6). Christ hath done it; that is the first thing, but that is not all.

(2.) He entered into heaven in our very names, and so is to be considered in that act as a common person (as well as in his death and resurrection), and so representing us, and also taking possession in our right, and we in him, as a guardian takes possession for heirs under age. Heb. 6:20, 'The forerunner is for us entered' into heaven; 'the forerunner for us', that is, our forerunner. A forerunner is a forerunner of followers, and of such as stay not long behind, and usually goes before as a harbinger, to provide and take up lodgings for them that are to come, and writes the names of those who are to come over the doors of such and such rooms, that they may not be taken up by any other. And so, Heb. 12:23, the names of 'the first-born' are said to be 'written in heaven', or enrolled there; and, 1 Pet. 1:4, their places or mansions in heaven are said to be 'reserved for them'; they stand empty as it were, yet taken up, so as none shall take them from them; their names and titles to them being entered and superscribed. And so he truly entered, *pro nobis*, for us, that is, in our stead and in our names, as a common person; and therefore the high priest (in the type) entered into the holy of holies, with all the names of the tribes on his breast; even so doth Christ with ours, even as a common person in our names, thereby showing that we are likewise to come after him; and this is more than simply to prepare a place, it is to take possession of a place, and give us a right thereto.

So that your faith, through this consideration, may see yourselves as good as in heaven already; for Christ is entered as a common person for you. Justification hath two parts: first, acquittance from sin and freedom from condemnation, as here, 'Who shall condemn?'

and secondly, 'justification of life', as it is called, Rom. 5:18, that is, which gives title to eternal life. Now dying and rising as a common person for us, procures the first, sets us perfectly enough in that state of freedom from condemnation. But then, this Christ, his entering into heaven as a common person, sets us far above that state of non-condemnation. It placeth us in heaven with him. You would think yourselves secure enough if you were ascended into heaven. As Heman said of his condition, that he was 'free among the dead', Psa. 88:5, that is, he reckoned himself (in his despair) free of the company in hell, as well as if he had been there; thinking his name enrolled among them and his place taken up. So you may 'reckon yourselves' (as the word is, Rom. 6) free of the company of heaven, and your places taken up there; so that when you come to die, you shall go to heaven as to your own place, by as true a title, though not of your own, as Judas went to hell, which is called 'his own place', as the apostle speaks, Acts 1. What a start is this! How far have you left below you pardon of sins and non-condemnation! You are got above. How securely may you say, 'Who shall condemn?' Christ hath ascended and entered into heaven. This is the first branch of the second head: the influence that Christ's ascension hath into our justification and salvation.

[Sect. 4]

Chapter 5

Demonstrateth in like manner what influence Christ's sitting at God's right hand hath into our justification, upon that second consideration of his being a common person. And the security faith may have from thence.

2. The consideration of his *sitting* at God's right hand may, in respect of the influence that it must needs have into our salvation, yet add more security unto our faith, if we either consider the power and authority of the place itself, and what it is to sit at God's right hand; or secondly, the relation, the person he bears and sustains in his sitting there, even of a common person in our right. And both these being put together will add strength mutually each to other, and unto our faith; both to consider how great a prerogative it is to sit at God's right hand, and what such a one as sits there hath power to do; and then that Christ (who is invested with this power, and advanced to it), he possesseth it all as our head, and in our right, as a common person representing us. And

(1.) Consider the prerogatives of the place itself; they are two:

[1.] Sovereignty of *power*, and might, and majesty.

[2.] Sovereignty of *authority* and judgment; either of which may secure us from non-condemnation.

[1.] Sovereignty of power and might; this the phrase 'sitting at God's right hand' implies, Matt. 26:64, where Christ himself expounded the purport of it: 'Hereafter you shall see the Son of man sitting on the right hand *of power*.' And so, Eph. 1:20, 22, this is made the privilege of God's 'setting him at his right hand', verse 20, that 'he hath put all things under his feet', verse 22 — a phrase importing the highest sovereignty and power, not used of any creatures, angels, or men; none of them have other things under their feet, *i.e.*, in so low a subjection as to be their vassals; especially, not *all* things; and therefore by that very phrase, 'the putting all things under his feet', the apostle argues in Heb. 2, that that man of whom David in the 8th Psalm (there cited by him) had spoken, was no other but Christ; not Adam, nor the angels, for to neither of these hath God subjected all things, verse 5, but to Christ only, verse 8, who sits in the highest throne of majesty. And to make his seat the easier, hath a world of enemies made his footstool, even all his enemies (so Psa. 110); which is the highest triumph in the world. Now to what end hath God committed this power to him, but that himself may be his own executor, and administrator, and perform all the legacies which he made to those whom he died for? As the expression is, Heb. 9:15-17, that none of his heirs might be wronged. Fairer dealing than this could there ever be, nor greater security given to us. This to have been God's very end of investing Christ with this sovereign power, is declared by Christ himself, John 17:2, 'Thou hast given him power over all flesh, that he should give eternal life to as many as thou hast given him.' And accordingly at his ascension, to comfort his disciples, in the fruit of their ministry, Matt. 28:18, he says, 'All power is given to me in heaven and in earth.' What holy confidence may this breed in us! He is at God's right hand, and we are in his hands, John 10:28, and all his enemies are under his feet, who then can pull us out? Rev. 1:18, says Christ, 'I have the keys of hell and death.' The key is still in the Scripture phrase the ensign of power and authority. Now Christ hath both the keys of death, the postern gate[1] out of this world, and of hell, even of the broad gates of that eternal prison; so as none of his can be fetched out of this world by death, but Christ he must first open the door; much less can any go to hell without his warrant. Yea, Matt. 16:19, he hath 'the keys of the kingdom of heaven' also, to open to whom he will. By his resurrection, we may see and

---

[1] back door or rear gate.—P.

rest assured that he hath the keys of death and hell (for he unlocked the doors, and came out from thence), and by his ascension and sitting at God's right hand, that he hath the keys of heaven, whose door he hath unlocked, and now set open. What need we then fear hell, when Christ our Redeemer hath the keys of it?

[2.] Secondly, to sit at God's right hand, imports all judgment to be committed to him; for sitting was a posture of judges; a phrase used to note out their authority. So Prov. 20:8, 'A king that sitteth on the throne of judgment, scattereth the wicked with his eye'; and so doth Christ his and our enemies. See what Christ says, John 5:21, 22, 'The Son of man raiseth up whom he will; for the Father judgeth no man, but hath committed all judgment to the Son.' Now if he who loved us so, and died for us, be the Judge himself, then, 'Who shall condemn?' Christ sits on God's right hand. This is the very inference that after followeth, verse 24, of that 5th chapter of John, 'He that believes shall not come into condemnation.' Christ utters it upon his having said he had all judgment committed to him, in the foregoing, verse 22, on purpose that he might from that consideration ascertain believers of their non-condemnation. For what need we fear any under-officers, when we have the Judge thus for us?

(2.) But then, in the last place, add that second particular mentioned to all these, that Christ sits there as an head, as a common person for us. First as an head; so Eph. 1, when the apostle had so hyperbolically set forth his power, of being advanced unto God's right hand, verse 21, 'far above all principalities and powers, and above every name that is named, not only in this world, but that which is to come'; and how God 'hath put all things under his feet'; he adds, 'and hath given him to be head over all things to the church'. Observe now, he is said to sit there over all things, not in his own pure personal right simply, as it is his inheritance, as he is the Son of God (as Heb. 1:3-5, it is affirmed of him), but he sits thus over all as a head to the church. That same *over all things* comes, in there, between his being an *head*, and *to the church,* on purpose to show that he is set over all, in relation to his church. So that we see that our relation is involved, and our right included, in this exaltation of his, and so put into his commission; for this prerogative is there said to be given him. He sits not simply as a Son, but as an head; and he sits not as an head without a body, and therefore must have his members up to him. Wherefore in the next verse it is added, 'which is his body, yea, his fullness'; so as Christ is not complete without all his members, and would leave heaven if any one were wanting. It were a lame, maimed body, if it wanted but a toe. Christ is our element,[1] and he being ascended, we are sparks that fly upwards to him. He took our flesh, and carried it into heaven, and left us his Spirit on earth, and both as pawns[2] and earnests that we should follow.

Nay, further yet, he is not only said to sit as our head, but we are also said 'to sit together with him'. That is made the upshot of all in the next chapter, Eph. 2:6. So that as we arose with him, he being considered as a common person, and ascended with him, as was said; so yet further, we 'sit together with him in the highest heavens' (as there), ἐν τοῖς ἐπουρανίοις [*en tois epouraniois*], *in supercœlestibus*, 'in his exalted estate above the heavens', as is the meaning of that phrase; not that Christ being at God's right hand (if taken for that sublimity of power) is communicable to us; that is Christ's prerogative only. So Heb. 1:13, 'To which of all the angels did he ever say, Sit thou at my right hand?' Yet so as his sitting in heaven, as it is indefinitely expressed, is understood to be as in our right and stead, and as a common person, and

---

[1] The reference is to the old idea of the four elements occupying their several places, one above the other; which was supposed to be the reason why stones fall, and rivers run into the sea, and flames rise. — Ed.

[2] An item given as a security for payment or performance. — P.

so is to assure us of our sitting there with him, in our proportion; so, Rev. 3:21, it is expressly rendered as the mind and intendment of it, 'Him that overcometh, I will grant to sit with me in my throne, even as I also am set down with my Father in his throne.' There is a proportion observed, though with an inequality; we sit on Christ's throne, but he only on his Father's throne; that is, Christ only sits at God's right hand, but we, on Christ's right hand; and so the church is said to be at Christ's 'right hand', Psa. 45:9. Yea, further (and it may afford a farther comfort to us in the point in hand), this represents, that at the latter day we shall sit as assessors on his judgment-seat, to judge the world with him. So Matt. 19:28, and Luke 22:30, 'When the Son of man shall sit in his glory, ye shall sit upon twelve thrones, judging the tribes of Israel.' So as this our sitting with him, it is spoken in respect to judgment, and to giving the sentence of it; not a sentence shall pass without your votes. So as you may by faith not only look on yourselves as already in heaven, sitting with Christ, as a common person, in your right, but you may look upon yourselves as judges also; so that if any sin should arise to accuse or condemn, yet it must be with your votes. And what greater security can you have than this? For you must condemn yourselves, if you be condemned; you may very well say, 'Who shall accuse? Who shall condemn?' for you will never pronounce a fatal sentence upon your own selves.

As then Paul triumphed here, so may we; for at the present we sit in heaven with Christ, and have all our enemies under our feet. As Joshua made his servants set their feet on the necks of those five kings; so God would have us by faith to do the like to all ours; for one day we shall do it. And if you say, We see it not, I answer, as Heb. 2, the apostle saith of Christ himself, 'Now we see not yet all things put under him', verse 8, now not under him, for he now sits in heaven, and *expects*, by faith, when his enemies shall be made his footstool, as Heb. 10:12th and 13th verses; 'but we see' for the present 'Jesus crowned with glory and honour', verse 9, and so may be sure that the thing is as good as done; and we may, in seeing him thus crowned, see ourselves sitting with him, and quietly wait and expect, as Christ himself doth, till all be accomplished, and our salvation finished and fully perfected.

His intercession now remains only to be spoken of, which yet will afford further considerations to strengthen our faith. His sitting at God's right hand notes out his power over all, from God; but his intercession, all power and favour with God for us; so as to effect our salvation for us, with God's highest contentment and good will, and all yet further to secure us. 'Who shall condemn?' *etc.*

SECTION 5

THE TRIUMPH OF FAITH FROM CHRIST'S INTERCESSION

Who also maketh intercession for us.
ROM. 8:34.

Chapter 1

A connection of this with the former; and how this adds a further support.—Two things out of the text propounded to be handled: First, the concurrency of influence that Christ's intercession hath into our salvation. Secondly, the security that faith may have therefrom for our justification.

We have seen Christ sitting at God's right hand as a judge and king, having all authority of saving or condemning in his own hands; and having all power in heaven and earth to give eternal life to them that believe; and the confidence that this giveth us.

Let us now come to his *intercession*, and the influence which it hath into our justification and salvation; which as it strikes the last stroke to make all sure, so as great a stroke as any of the former; therefore, as you have heard that there was an all-sufficiency in his death—'Who shall condemn? It is Christ that died'—a *rather* in his resurrection—'yea rather, is risen again'—a much rather (πολλῷ μᾶλλον [*pollo mallon*]), that he lives and is at God's right hand,

Rom. 5:10. The apostle riseth yet higher to an εἰς τὸ παντελὲς [*eis to panteles*], 'a saving to the utmost', put upon his intercession; Heb. 7:25, 'Wherefore he is able to save to the utmost, seeing he ever lives to make intercession.' So that if you could suppose there were anything which none of all the former three could do or effect for us, yet his intercession could do it to the utmost, for itself is the uttermost and highest. If money would purchase our salvation, his death hath done it, which he laid down as a price and an equivalent ransom (as it is in 1 Tim. 2:6). If power and authority would effect it, his sitting at God's right hand, invested with all power in heaven and earth, shall be put forth to the utmost to effect it. If favour and entreaties added to all these (which ofttimes doth as much as any of those other) were needful, he will use the utmost of this also, and for ever make intercession. So that if love, money, or power (any of them, or all of them) will save us, we shall be sure to be saved, 'saved to the utmost', εἰς τὸ παντελὲς [*eis to panteles*], all manner of ways, by all manner of means; saved over and over.

For the clearing of this last general head, the intercession of Christ, and the influence and security it hath into our faith and justification, I shall handle two things, and both proper to the text.

1. First, show how unto all those other fore-mentioned acts of Christ for us, this of intercession also is to be added by him for the effecting our salvation, and the securing our hearts therein. This that particle *also* in the text calls for, 'Who *also* maketh intercession for us.'

2. Then secondly, to show the security that faith may assume and fetch from this intercession of Christ, or his praying for us in heaven; 'Who shall condemn? It is Christ that maketh intercession for us.'

Chapter 2

The first head explained by two things: First, Intercession one part of Christ's priesthood, and the most excellent part of it.

1. Towards the explanation of the first of these, two things arc to be done.

(1.) First, To show how great, and necessary, and how excellent a part of Christ's priesthood his intercession and praying for us in heaven is.

(2.) Secondly, To show the peculiar influence that intercession hath into our salvation, and so the reasons for which God ordained this work of intercession for us, and that in heaven, to be added to all the former.

(1.) For the first I will proceed therein by degrees.

[1.] It is one part of his priesthood. You must know that Christ is not entered into heaven simply as a 'forerunner' (which hath been explained) to take up places for you, but as a priest also: 'made a priest, after the order of Melchisedec', which is more than simply a forerunner. Yea, his sitting at God's right hand is not only as a king armed with power and authority to save us, but he sits there as a priest too: Thus, Heb. 8:1, 'We have such an High Priest, who is set down at the right hand of the Majesty on high.'

In the old Levitical priesthood, the high priest's office had two parts, both which concurred to make them high priests.

First, Oblation, or offering the sacrifice.

Secondly, Presentation of it in the holy of holies, with prayer and intercession unto God, to accept it for the sins of the people. The one was done *without*, the other *within* the holy of holies. This you see in many places, especially Lev. 16:11, 15, 16, where you have the law about the high priest's entering into the holy of holies; he was not to come into the holy place till first he had offered a sacrifice for himself and the people, verses 11 and 15, and this *without*. Then, secondly, when he had killed it, he was to enter with the blood of it *into* the holy of holies, and sprinkle the mercy-seat therein with it, verses 14, 17, and to go with incense, and cause a cloud to arise over the mercy-seat. And this you have also, Heb. 13:11, it is said, that the blood of those beasts that were burnt without the camp was brought into the sanctuary by the high priest; and in that 16th of Leviticus you shall find the atonement made as well by the blood, when brought into the holy place, verse 16, as by the killing of the beast, verse 11. Both these were acts of the high priesthood for atonement.

And this was done in a type and of the priestly office of Christ, and the parts thereof. So, Heb. 9:23, he calls all those transactions under the ceremonial law, 'the patterns of things heavenly'; instancing in this part of Christ's office, verse 24, 'For Christ', says he, 'is not entered into the holy places made with hands', as that was, 'which are the figures of the true, but into heaven itself, to appear in the presence of God for us.' Now, then, in answer to this type, there are two distinct parts of Christ's priesthood.

First, The 'offering himself a sacrifice' up to death, as Heb. 9:26, which answers to the killing of the sacrifice without the holy of holies; for answerably he was crucified without the city, Heb. 13:12.

Secondly, He carried this his blood into the holy of holies, namely, the heavens, Heb. 9:12, where he appears, verse 24, and there also prays in the force of that blood. And the type of those prayers was that cloud of incense made by the high priest; so it is expressly interpreted, Rev. 8:3, *etc.* The angel Christ is said to have had 'much incense to offer with the prayers of all the saints'. Which incense is his own prayers in heaven, which he continually puts up when the saints pray on earth, and so perfumes all their prayers, and procures all blessings for them.

Both these parts of his priesthood the Apostle John mentions in his First Epistle, chap. 2, verse 2, where, as he calls Jesus Christ a 'propitiation for our sins' (that is, an oblation or sacrifice offered up for us); so likewise he calls him our advocate, both going to make up this his office. And, indeed, this latter of intercession, and bringing his blood into the holy of holies (or heaven), is but the same action continued. That blood which he offered with tears and strong cries on the cross, where he likewise interceded, the same blood he continues virtually to offer up with prayers in the heavens, and makes atonement by both, only with this difference; on earth, though he interceded, yet he more eminently offered up himself; in heaven, he more eminently intercedes, and doth but present that offering.

[2.] Secondly, this was so necessary a part of his priesthood, that without it he had not been a complete priest. Thus, Heb. 8:4, 'If he were on earth he should not be a priest'; that is, if he should have abode on earth he should not have been a complete priest. Paul saith not, that if he had offered that his sacrifice on earth, he had not been a priest, for that was necessary; but that if he had stayed still on earth, after he had offered it, he had not been a priest, that is, a perfect priest; for he had then left his office imperfect, and had done it but by halves, seeing this other part of it (the work of intercession) lay still upon him to be acted in heaven. Thus the high priest, his type, if he had only offered sacrifice without the holy of holies, had not been a perfect high priest; for to enter into the holy of holies, and to act the part of a priest there, was the proper, peculiar work of the high priest as such. Which shows, that Christ had not been an high priest if he had not gone to heaven, and priested it there too, as I may so speak, as well as upon earth. Yea, if Christ had not gone to heaven, and were not now become a priest there, then the Levitical priesthood were still in force, and should share the honour with him; and the high priest must continue still to go into the holy of holies. To this purpose you may observe, that so long as Christ was on earth, though risen, the types of the law held in force, and were not to give way, till all the truth signified by their ministry was fully accomplished; and so, not until Christ was gone into heaven as a priest, and there had begun to do all that which the high priest had done in the holy of holies, and as his type fore-signified. And this is plainly the meaning of what follows (in that Heb. 8:4) as the reason or demonstration why that Christ should not have been a priest, if he had not gone to heaven, not only as a king, but as a priest too, as he had affirmed, verse 4, 'Seeing', says he, 'that there are priests upon earth that do offer gifts according to the law.' The force of the reason lies thus: there are already priests, and that of a tribe he was not of, that offer gifts on earth, therefore he came into the world. And, therefore, if that had been all his priesthood, to be a priest on earth, they would plead possession before him, having been priests before him. And then he further backs his reason by this, that 'those priests served' (as it follows, verse 5), 'unto the example and shadow of heavenly things'. And, therefore, it is only a real priesthood in heaven which must put them out of place; and till such a priesthood comes, they must serve still, for the truth, which these serve to shadow out, is not till then fulfilled. This you have also, chap. 9:8. The 'first tabernacle' was to stand until a priest went into heaven, and did act that office there; so that, if Christ will be a priest alone, he must become a priest interceding in heaven; or else high priests must come up again, and share that office with him; and so he should as good as fall from his office, and lose all that he had done.

[3.] Yea, thirdly, this part of his priesthood is of the two the more eminent, yea, the top, the height of his priesthood. And this is held forth to us in the types of both those two orders of priesthood that were before him, and figures of him, both that of Aaron and Melchisedec: *First*, This was typified out in that Levitical priesthood of Aaron and his fellows: the highest service of that office was the going into the holy of holies, and making an atonement there; yea, this was the height of the high priest's honour, that he did this alone, and did constitute the difference between him, as he was high priest, and other priests; for they killed and offered the sacrifices without as well as he, every ordinary priest did that; but none but the high priest was to approach the holy of holies with blood, and this but once a-year. Thus, Heb. 9:6, 7, 'the priests', namely those inferior priests, 'went always', that is, daily, morning and evening, 'into the first tabernacle', or court of priests, which was without the holy of holies, 'accomplishing the service of God'; namely, that offering of the daily sacrifice; 'but into the second', namely, the holy of holies, 'went the *high priests* alone every year'. So, then, this was that high and transcendent prerogative of that high priest then, and which indeed made him high priest; and answerably the height of our high priest's office,—although he alone also could offer a satisfactory sacrifice, as the apostle shows, Heb. 9 and 10,—yet comparatively lay in this, that he entered into the heavens by his blood, and is set down on the majesty on high, and in the virtue of his sacrifice there doth intercede. I know but one place that calleth him the 'Great High Priest' (higher before than Aaron), and that is Heb. 4:14. And then it is in this respect that he is 'passed into the heavens', as it follows there.

Secondly, The excellency of this part of his priesthood was likewise typified out by Melchisedec's priesthood, which the apostle argueth to have been much more excellent than that of Aaron's, inasmuch as Levi, Aaron's father, paid tithes to this Melchisedec in Abraham's loins. Now Melchisedec was his type, not so much in respect of his oblation, or offering of sacrifice (that work which Christ performed on earth), but in respect of that work which he ever performs in heaven: therefore that same clause *for ever* still comes in, in the quotation and mention of Melchisedec's priesthood in that epistle; because in respect of that his continual intercession in heaven, Melchisedec was properly Christ's type. And accordingly you may observe, Psa. 110, when is it that speech comes in, 'Thou art a priest for ever after the order of Melchisedec', but then, when God had him sitting at his right hand? verse 1. So that, as the transcendent excellency of Christ's priesthood was typified out by Melchisedec's rather than Aaron's, as being the better priesthood of the two, so this, the most excellent part thereof, was typified out thereby, namely, that which Christ for ever acteth in heaven.

And, *thirdly*, to confirm this, you shall find this to be made the top notion of this Epistle to the Hebrews, and the scope of it chiefly, to discourse of Christ's eternal priesthood in heaven, and to show how therein Melchisedec was a type of him. This is not only expressed both in Heb. 7:21 and 25, where this same *for ever* is applied to his intercession, verse 25, but more expressly in chap. 8:1, where the apostle puts the emphasis upon this part of his priesthood, saying, that 'of the things which we have spoken',—or which are to be spoken, for the word ἐπὶ τοῖς λεγομένοις [*epi tois legomenois*] will bear either,—'this is', says he, 'the sum or argument' of all: the word is κεφάλαιον [*kephalaion*], and signifies as well the *head*, the *chief*, the *top* of all, and above all, as it doth the sum of all. And what is it that he thus professeth to be both the main subject and argument of this epistle, and the top and eminent thing in Christ he intends to discourse of? It follows, that 'we have such an high priest as is set down at the right hand of the throne of the Majesty in the heavens'. And of the priestly office he alone discourseth both before and after; and in the following verses calleth his ministry or office (in respect of this) 'a more excellent ministry', verse 6, 'he being such a priest as was higher than the heavens', as he had set him out in the latter part of the former chapter. And therefore you may observe, how in his preface to this Epistle to the Hebrews, in chap. 1, verse 3, he holds up this to our eye as the argument of the whole saying, 'When he had by himself purged our sins, he sat down on the right hand of the Majesty on high.'

Yea, to conclude this, all his priesthood would have been ineffectual, if he had not acted the part of a priest in heaven, by intercession there; for by his death he did but begin the execution of his office: in heaven he ends it; and if he had not fulfilled his office in both, the work of our salvation had not been fully perfected; it was therefore as necessary as oblation itself. Not but that his death was a perfect oblation; it was perfect for an oblation, to which as such nothing can be added. There needed no more, nor any other price to be paid for us; 'by that one offering, he perfects us for ever', as Heb. 10:14, and became himself perfect thereby, Heb. 5:9. And in the 9th chapter, verse 12, 'By his own blood he entered into the holy place, having obtained eternal redemption for us.' Mark how before he entered by his blood into heaven, he had fully *obtained* a redemption, and that eternal, that is, for ever sufficient; which done, he became through his intercession in heaven an applying cause of eternal salvation, as Heb. 5:9, 10, hath it. So that as in his death he paid the full sum of all he owed; unto which payment nothing can be added, no not by himself, though he would come and die again; it was made at that *once* as perfect, that is, for an oblation, as ever himself could make. But yet still by God's ordination there remained another further action of another kind that was to be added to this of oblation, and that is, intercession, or praying for us in heaven; otherwise our salvation by his death were not perfected; for if his priesthood be imperfect, our salvation then must needs be so. The presenting of that his sacrifice in heaven, was the consummation of his priesthood, and the performance of that part there, the perfection of it.

Chapter 3

The second; the special peculiar influence that intercession
hath into our salvation and justification, and the reasons
why God appointed it to be added to the former.

2. To come now more particularly to show that
proper and special influence that intercession hath
into our salvation, and what it adds to the oblation of Christ's death, though in its kind perfect, in
order to the effecting our salvation; and to show the
more inward reasons why God ordained—for upon
his ordination alone this is to be put—this work of
intercession in heaven to be joined with his death.
And both these I shall put promiscuously together;
for in laying down the *reasons* why God thus ordered
our salvation to be brought about by it, that *influence*
also which intercession hath into our salvation, will
together therewith appear.

The reasons either respect (1.) God himself, who
will have us so saved as himself may be most glorified;
or (2.) respect us and our salvation; God ordering
all the links of this golden chain of the causes of our
salvation, as should make our salvation most sure
and stedfast (as David in his last song speaks, 2 Sam.

23:5). Or (3.) respect Christ himself, whose glory is to be held up, and throughout continued as the author and finisher of our salvation, beginner and ender of our faith and justification.

(1.) The first sort of reasons respect God himself.

[1.] In general, God will be dealt withal like himself, in and throughout the whole way of our salvation, from first to last, and carry it all along as a superior wronged, and so keep a distance between himself and sinners; who still are to come to him by a priest, and a mediator (as Heb. 7:25 hath it) upon whose mediation and intercession 'for ever', as there, at least till the day of judgment, their salvation doth depend; and therefore though Christ, in his dispensation of all to us downward, doth carry it as a *king*, as one having all power to justify and condemn (as hath been shown), yet upward, towards God, he carries it as a *priest*, who must still intercede to do all that which he has power to do as a king. Therefore in the second Psalm, after that God had set him up as 'king upon his holy hill', verse 6, namely, in heaven, and so had committed all power in heaven and earth to him; then he must yet 'ask' all that he would have done; 'Ask of me, and I will give thee', *etc.,* verse 8, says God to him; for though he be a king, yet he is God's king, 'I have set *my* king', *etc.,* and by asking him, God will be acknowledged to be above him. But more of this hereafter. But

[2.] More particularly. God hath two attributes which he would have most eminently appear in their highest glory by Christ's effecting our salvation, namely, justice and free grace; and therefore hath so ordered the bringing about of our salvation, as that Christ must apply himself in a more especial manner unto each of these, by way of satisfaction to the one, of entreaty to the other. Justice will be known to be justice, and dealt with upon its own terms; and grace will be acknowledged to be free grace, throughout the accomplishment of our salvation. You have both these joined, Rom. 3:24, 26, 'Being justified *freely through his grace*, by the *redemption* that is in Christ Jesus; that he might be just, and the justifier of him that believes.' Here is highest justice and the freest grace both met to save us, and both ordained by God to be 'declared' and 'set forth', as verse 25 and 26 have it. I said before, that God justifies and saves us through free grace, so absolutely freely, as if his justice had had no satisfaction. Now therefore our salvation depending and being carried on, even in the application of it, by a continuation of grace in a free way, notwithstanding satisfaction unto justice, therefore this free grace must be sought to, and treated with like itself, and applied upon in all, and the sovereignty and freeness of it acknowledged in all, even as well as God's justice had the honour to be satisfied by a price paid upon it, that so the severity of it might appear and be held forth in our salvation. Thus God having two attributes eminently to be dealt withal, his justice and his free grace, it was meet that there should be two eminent actions of Christ's priesthood, wherein he should apply himself to each according to their kind, and as the nature and glory of each doth require. And accordingly in his death he deals with justice, by laying down a sufficient price; and in his intercession, he entreateth free grace, and thus both come to be alike acknowledged. In Heb. 4:16, we are encouraged to 'come boldly to the throne of grace', because 'we have an high priest entered into the heavens'. Observe how it is called a *throne of grace*, which our high priest now in heaven officiates at; so called because his priesthood there deals with free grace chiefly, it is a throne of grace, and so to be sued unto; therefore he treateth with God by way of intercession. Of this throne of grace in heaven, the mercy-seat in the holy of holies was the type. And as there the high priest was to bring the blood and mercy-seat together, he was to sprinkle the blood upon it, so Christ. And as the high priest was to go into the holy of holies by blood, so with incense also (that is, prayer), to show that heaven is not opened by mere justice, or bringing only a price in hand for it, but by grace also, and that must be entreated; and therefore when the priest was within that holy place, he was to make a cloud over the mercy-seat, which cloud of incense is prayer, whereof incense was the type, Rev. 8:3. And thence it is, that Christ hath as much work of it still in heaven as ever, though of another kind. He dealt with justice here below, to satisfy it, and here got money enough to pay the debt; but in heaven he deals with mercy. Therefore all the grace he bestows on us, he is said first to receive it, even now when in heaven. Acts 2:33, it is said of him, after his going to heaven, and that he was exalted, *etc.*, that he 'received the promise of the Spirit', which John 14:16, he told them he would 'pray for'. And this is part of the meaning of that in Psa. 68:18, 'He ascended up on high, and received gifts for men', says the Psalmist. The apostle renders it, Eph. 4, 'gave', but you see it was by 'receiving' them first, as fruits of his intercession and asking after his ascending. He is said both to give, as being all of his own purchase, and as having power as a king also both to do and bestow all he doth; and yet withal he is said to receive all that he gives, because as a priest he intercedes for it, and asks it. Free grace requires this. This is the first thing.

Yea, secondly, justice itself might stand a little upon it, though there was enough in Christ his death to satisfy it; yet having been wronged, it stood thus far upon it, as those to whom a debt is due use to do, namely, to have the money brought home to God's dwelling-house, and laid down there. God is resolved not to stoop one whit unto man, no nor to Christ his surety. Justice will not only be satisfied, and have a sufficient ransom collected and paid, as at Christ's death, but he must come and bring his bags up to heaven; justice will be paid it upon the mercy-seat; for so in the type the blood was to be carried into the holy of holies, and sprinkled upon the mercy-seat. And therefore his resurrection, ascension, *etc.*, were but as the breaking through all enemies, and subduing them, to the end to bring this price or satisfaction to the mercy-seat; and so God having his money by him, might not want wherewithal to pardon sinners; so as the blood of Christ is current money, not only on earth, but in heaven too, whither all is brought, which is for our comfort, that all the treasure which should satisfy God is safely conveyed thither, and our surety with it.

(2.) The second sort of reasons why God ordained Christ's intercession to be joined to his death, are taken from what was the best way to effect and make sure our salvation, and secure our hearts therein; and these reasons will show the peculiar influence that intercession hath into our salvation, and therein as in the former.

[1.] First in general, God would have our salvation made sure, and us saved all manner of ways, over and over. *First*, By ransom and price (as captives are redeemed), which was done by his death, which of itself was enough; for it is said, Heb. 10, to 'perfect us for ever'. *Secondly*, By power and rescue; so in his resurrection, and ascension, and sitting at God's right hand, which also was sufficient. Then, *thirdly*, again by intercession, a way of favour and entreaty; and this likewise would have been enough, but God would have all ways concur in it, whereof notwithstanding not one could fail; a threefold cord, whereof each twine were strong enough, but all together must of necessity hold.

[2.] Secondly, the whole application of his remedy, both in justifying and saving of us first and last, hath a special dependence upon this his intercession. This all divines on all sides do attribute unto it, whilst they put this difference between the influence of his death, and that of his intercession into our salvation: calling his death *medium impetrationis*, that is, the means of

procurement or obtaining it for us; but his intercession *medium applicationis*, the means of applying all
unto us. Christ purchaseth salvation by the one, but
possesseth us of it by the other. Some have attributed
the application of justification to his resurrection; but
it is much more proper to ascribe it to his intercession (and what causal influence his resurrection hath
into our justification, hath been afore in the third
section declared). But that his eternal priesthood in
heaven, and the work of its intercession, is the applying cause of our eternal salvation, in all the parts of
it, first and last, seems to me to be the result of the
connection of the 8th, 9th, and 10th verses of the
5th chapter to the Hebrews. For having spoken of
his obedience and sufferings unto death, verse 8, and
how he thereby was made perfect, verse 9, he says,
'and being' thus first 'made perfect, he became the
author' or applying cause, αἴτιος [*aitios*], 'of eternal
salvation, unto all them that obey him'; and this by
his being become an eternal priest in heaven, after
he was thus perfected by sufferings; for so it follows,
verse 10, 'called of God an high priest, after the order
of Melchisedec'. And Melchisedec's priesthood was
principally the type of his priesthood in heaven, as
was before declared. One leading instance to show
that his intercession was to be the applying cause

of salvation, was given by Christ, whilst he was on earth, thereby manifesting what much more was to be done by him in heaven, through his intercession there; when he was on the cross, and as then offering that great sacrifice for sin, he at that time also joined prayers for the justification of those that crucified him, 'Father forgive them, for they know not what they do'; so fulfilling that in Isa. 53:12, 'He bare the sins of many, and made intercession for the transgressors.' And the efficacy of that prayer then put up, was the cause of the conversion of those three thousand, Acts 2, whom, verse 23, the apostle had expressly charged with the crucifying of Christ, 'whom ye by wicked hands have taken, crucified, and slain'. These were the first-fruits of his intercession, whose prayers still do reap and bring in the rest of the crop, which in all ages is to grow up unto God on earth.

[3.] And more particularly, as the whole application in general, so our justification, in the whole progress of it, depends upon Christ's intercession. As,

First, Our first actual or initial justification, which is given us at our first conversion, depends upon Christ's intercession. Therefore in the fore-mentioned prayer on the cross, the thing he prayed for was forgiveness, 'Father, forgive them.' You heard before that Christ's death affords the matter of our justification, as being that which is imputed, the ransom, the price, the thing itself that satisfies; and that his resurrection was the original act of God's justifying us in Christ. We were virtually justified then in Christ his being justified, as in a common person. But besides all this, there is a personal or an actual justification to be bestowed upon us, that is, an accounting and bestowing it upon us in our own persons, which is done when we believe, and it is called (Rom. 5:1), a being 'justified by faith', and (verse 11), 'received the atonement'; now this depends on Christ's intercession, and it was typified out by Moses his sprinkling the people with blood, mentioned Heb. 9:19, which thing Jesus Christ as a Mediator and Priest doth now from heaven. For, Heb. 12:23, 24, it is said, 'You are come to heaven, and to Jesus the Mediator of the new covenant, and', as it is next subjoined, 'to the blood of sprinkling.' He shed his blood on the cross on earth, but he sprinkleth it now as a priest from heaven. For it is upon Mount Zion, to which (he had said first in the former verse) ye are come; and so to Christ as a mediator standing on that mount, and sprinkling from thence his blood; and so therein there is an allusion unto Moses, Christ's type, who sprinkled the people with the blood of that ceremonial covenant, the type of the covenant of grace. Now, in 1 Pet. 1:2, 'The sprinkling of his blood', as it is there made the more proper work of Christ himself, in distinction from the other persons, and therefore was done by Moses, who was his type, so is it also put for our first justification. And this sprinkling, as it is there mentioned, is from the virtue of his intercession. And therefore in that place of the Hebrews fore-cited, he attributes an intercession unto it, as the phrase that follows, 'which speaks better things', *etc.*, doth imply, of which more hereafter. Yet concerning this first head, let me add this by way of caution (which I shall presently have occasion to observe), that though this our first justification is to be ascribed to his intercession, yet more eminently intercession is ordained for the accomplishing our salvation, and this other more rarely in the Scripture attributed thereunto.

Secondly, The continuation of our justification depends upon it. And as his intercession is the virtual continuation of his sacrifice, so is it the continuing cause of our justification; which though it be an act done once, as fully as ever, yet is it done over every moment, for it is continued by acts of free grace, and so renewed actually every moment. There is a 'standing in grace' by Christ, spoken of Rom. 5:2, as well as a first 'access by Christ', and that standing in grace, and continuing in it, is afterwards, verse 10, attributed to his life, that is, as it is interpreted, Heb. 7:25, his living ever to intercede. We owe our standing in grace every moment to his sitting in heaven and interceding every moment. There is no fresh act of justification goes forth, but there is a fresh act of intercession. And as though God created the world once for all, yet every moment he is said to create, every new act of providence being a new creation; so likewise to justify continually, through his continuing out free grace to justify as at first; and this Christ doth by continuing his intercession; he continues 'a priest for ever', and so we continue to be justified for ever.

Thirdly, There is hereby a full security given us of justification to be continued for ever. The danger either must lie in old sins coming into remembrance, or else from sins newly to be committed. Now, first, God hereby takes order, that no old sins shall come up into remembrance, to trouble his thought, as in the old law, after the priest's going into the holy of holies, their sins are said yet to have done, Heb. 10:3; and to that end it was that he placed Christ as his remembrancer for us, so near him, to take up his thoughts so with his obedience, that our sins might not come into mind. Not that God needed this help to put himself in mind, but only for a formality sake, that things being thus really carried between God and Christ for us, according to a way suiting with our apprehensions, our faith might be strengthened against all suppositions, and fears of after reviving our guilts. Look therefore as God ordained the rainbow in the heavens, that when he looked on it, he might remember his covenant, never to destroy the world again by water; so he hath set Christ as the rainbow about his throne. And look as the bread and wine in the Lord's supper are appointed on earth to 'show forth Christ's death', as a remembrancer to us; so is Christ himself appointed in heaven to show forth his death really as a remembrancer thereof to his Father; and indeed, the one is correspondent to the other. Only the papists have perverted the use of the Lord's supper, by making it on earth a commemorative sacrifice to God, whenas it is but a remembrancer thereof to men; and besides, their priests therein do take upon themselves this very office of presenting this sacrifice to God, which is proper only to Christ in heaven. But God, when he would make sure not to be tempted to remember our sins any more, nor trouble himself with them, hath set his Christ by him to put him in mind of his so pleasing an offering. So the high priest going into the holy of holies, was for a memorial, and therein the type of Christ. And this is plainly and expressly made the use of this execution of his priestly office in heaven, Heb. 8, where the apostle having discoursed of that part of his office, as the chief thing he aimed at in this epistle, verse 1, and of the necessity of it, verses 3-5, and excellency of it in this respect, verse 6, he then shows how from thence the new covenant of pardon came to be sure and stedfast, that God 'will remember our sins no more', verse 12, which he there brings in as the proper use of this doctrine, and of this part of his priesthood.

Secondly, As by reason of intercession God remembers not old sins, so likewise he is not provoked by new. For though God, when he justifies us, should forgive all old sins past for ever, so as never to remember them more, yet new ones would break forth, and he could not but take notice of them; and so, so long as sin continues, there is need of a continuing intercession. Therefore for the securing us in this, it is said, Rom. 5:10, that 'if, when we were enemies, we were reconciled to God by the death of his Son, much more, being reconciled, we shall be saved by his life'. Where we see that his death is in some more special manner said to procure reconciliation at first for sins of unregeneracy, and to bring us to Christ; but then his life and intercession, or living to intercede, is said to keep God and us friends, that we may never fall out more. What Christ did on earth, doth more especially procure reconciliation for sins which we do in the state of nature; so as notwithstanding them, God resolves to turn us from that state and draw us to Christ. But sins which we commit after conversion, though pardoned also by his death, yet the pardon of them is more especially attributed to his life and intercession, as a daily preservative, a continual plaster (as some call it) to heal such sins. So that it would seem that God out of his eternal love doth bring us to Christ, and draws us to him through the beholding the reconciliation wrought by his death, and so gives us at first conversion unto Christ; and we being brought to him, he sprinkles us with his blood; and then God says to him, Now do you look to them, that they and I fall out no more. And to that end Christ takes our cause in hand by that eternal priesthood of his, and from that time begins more especially to intercede for us. And thus sins after the state of grace may be said more eminently to be taken away by that part of his priesthood which he now in heaven performs. That place also, 1 John 2:1, 2, seems to make this the great end of intercession, 'If any man sin' (that is, if any of the company of believers, to whom alone he wrote), 'we have an advocate with the Father'; so as intercession principally serves for sins to come, or committed after grace received. Thus also in his prayer, John 17, which was left as a pattern of his intercession in heaven, he prays for his elect as believers, 'I pray for them that shall believe through their word.' Not but that sins after conversion are taken away by his death; and sins before it, by his intercession also; for Christ interceded for those who crucified him, and by virtue of that intercession, those three thousand were converted (as was observed). But the meaning only is, that yet more eminently the work of reconciliation for sins before conversion is attributed to his death; and for sins after conversion to his intercession. Even as the persons of the Trinity, though they have all a like hand in all the work of our salvation, yet we see that one part is attributed more to one person, and another to another.

(3.) A third sort of reasons why God ordained this work of intercession to accomplish our salvation by, do respect Christ himself, whose honour and glory, and the perpetuation of it in our hearts, God had as well in his eye in the ordering all the workings of our salvation, as much as his own, 'that all might honour the Son as well as the Father', as Christ himself speaks. Now, therefore, for the maintaining and upholding his glory, and the comings in thereof, did God ordain, after all that he had done for us here below, this work of intercession in heaven to be added to all the rest, for the perfecting of our salvation. As,

First, It became him, and was for his honour, that none of his offices should be vacant or lie idle, and he want employment in them. All offices have work to accompany them, and all work hath honour, as its reward, to arise out of it. And therefore when he had done all that was to be done on earth, as appertaining unto the merit of our salvation, he appoints this full and perpetual work in heaven, for the applying and possessing us of salvation, and that as a priest, by praying and interceding in the merit of that one oblation of himself. God would have Christ never to be out of office, nor out of work. And this very reason is more than intimated, Heb. 7:24. 'This man, because he continueth ever, hath an unchangeable priesthood' (or, as verse 21 expounds it) for ever. And the work of his priesthood is interpreted, verse 25, to be 'ever to make intercession'. The meaning is, that God would not have him continue to be a priest in title only, or in respect only of a service past, and so to have only the honour of priesthood perpetuated to him out of the remembrance of what he once had done, as great generals have, even in time of peace, the glory of some great battle fought, continued to them in their titles, or rewards for ever. But God would have him have, as the renown of the old, so a perpetual spring of honour by new work, and employment in that office which he is continually a-doing, so to preserve the verdure of his glory ever fresh and green, and therefore ordained a continual work for him. And the sum of the apostle's reasoning is this, that seeing himself was to be for ever, so should his work and priesthood be, that so his honour might be for ever. So verse 28 concludes it, 'consecrated or perfected for evermore'.

Secondly, For the same reason also, it became him that the whole work of our salvation, first and last, and every part of it, every step and degree of accomplishment of it, should be so ordered as he should continue still to have as great and continual a hand in every part, even to the laying of the top stone thereof, as he had in laying the first foundation and corner stone thereof. And this you have expressed, Heb. 12:2, 'Looking to Jesus the beginner and perfecter of our faith.' Two things had been said of him, as two causes of two effects; and we must look to him in both. [1.] He is to be looked at as dying, 'enduring the cross', as there he is set forth. [2.] As 'sitting at God's right hand and interceding', as that whole epistle had represented him. We are to look at these two as causes of a double effect, to look at his dying as that which is the 'beginning of our faith' (so according to the Greek, and the margin of our translation), and at his sitting at God's right hand as an intercessor, for the 'finishing of our faith' thereby; and so of our final salvation. For as Christ's work began in his life and death, which is put for all his obedience here below, so our first believing (as was said) begins by virtue of his death at first; and as his work ends in his intercession, and sitting at God's right hand, so answerably is our faith and salvation perfected by it, that thus he might be left out in nothing, but be 'the *Alpha* and *Omega*, the beginning and the ending, to whom be glory for ever'. So that we are to look upon our Mediator Christ, as doing as much work for us in heaven at this instant, as ever he did on earth; here suffering, but there praying and presenting his sufferings. All his work was not done, when he had done here; that work here was indeed the harder piece of the two, yet soon despatched; but his work in heaven, though sweeter far, yet lies on his hands for ever; therefore let us leave out none of these in our believing on him.

Chapter 4

*The second head: the great security the consideration of
Christ's intercession affords to faith for our justification,
showed, 1. By way of evidence; by two things.*

And so I come (as in the former I have done) to
show what strong grounds of security and triumph
our faith may raise from this last act, namely, Christ's
intercession for us in the point of justification; 'Who
shall condemn? It is Christ that intercedes.' And
was the second general propounded; and therein to
proceed also according to the method taken up in
the former.

1. What assurance by way of evidence this doth
afford unto faith of non-condemnation.

2. What powerful efficacy and influence this must
be of, that Christ intercedes.

1. First, to handle it by way of evidence.

That Christ intercedes, is a strong evidence to our
faith by two demonstrations.

(1.) From the very intent and scope of the work
of intercession itself, and what it is ordained by God
to effect.

(2.) From the end of Jesus Christ himself, who

lives in heaven on purpose to intercede for us. Our salvation it is both *finis operis*,[1] the end of the work, and *finis ipsius operantis*,[2] in some respect the end of Christ himself, the interceder; and both these do lay the greatest engagement that can be upon Christ, to accomplish our salvation through his intercession.

(1.) For the work itself. Intercession, you have seen, is a part of the office of Christ's priesthood, as well as his dying and offering himself: now all the works of Christ are and must be perfect in their kind (even as God's are, of which says Moses, Deut. 32:4, 'His work is perfect'), for otherwise he should not be a perfect priest. Now the perfection of every work lies in order to its end for which it is ordained; so as that work is perfect that attains to such an end as it is ordained for, and that imperfect which doth not. Now the immediate direct end of Christ's intercession is the actual salvation of believers elect, and persons whom he died for. The end of his death is *adoptio juris*,[3] purchasing a right unto salvation; but of intercession, *procuratio ipsius salutis*,[4] the very saving us actually, and putting us in possession of heaven. To this purpose, observe how the Scripture speaks concerning

[1] Latin: the end of the work. —P.
[2] Latin: the end of the actual worker. —P.
[3] Latin: assigning a right. —P.
[4] Latin: securing the actual salvation. —P.

Christ's death, Heb. 9:12, 'He entered into heaven, having obtained redemption', or found redemption, that is, by way of right, by procuring full title to it. But of his intercession it says, Heb. 7:25, that by it 'Christ is able to save to the utmost them that come unto God by him'; that is, actually to save, and put them in possession of happiness: that is made the end and scope of intercession there; and that phrase (εἰς τὸ παντελὲς [*eis to panteles*]), to the utmost, notes out a saving indeed, a doing it not by halves, but wholly, and throughly, and completely; εἰς τὸ παντελὲς [*eis to panteles*] is to save altogether, to give our salvation its last act and complement, that is the true force of the phrase, even to effect it, to the last of it, all that is to be done about it. Thus also Rom. 5:9, 10, 'We are justified by his death, but *saved* (namely, completely) by his life'; that is, his living to intercede. So that the very salvation of believers is it that is the work, the τὸ ἔργον [*to ergon*] of Christ's intercession.

Now what security doth this afford? For, to be saved is more than to be justified; for it is the actual possessing us of heaven. So then, do but grant that Christ's intercession is as perfect a work in its kind as Christ's death is in its kind, and you must needs be saved. The perfection of Christ's death, and the work thereof, wherein lay it (as on Christ's part to be performed) but in this, that he should lay down a ransom sufficient to purchase salvation for such and such persons as God would save? And so the perfection of it lies in the worth and sufficiency of it, to that end it was ordained for; it being a perfect sacrifice in itself, able to purchase eternal redemption for us, and to make us salvable against all sins and the demerits of them, and to give us right to heaven; and had it wanted a grain of this, it had then been imperfect. Now then, answerably for intercession, the comfort of our souls is, that the proper work that lies upon Christ therein is the complete saving those very persons, and the possessing them of heaven; this is the τὸ ἔργον [*to ergon*] the proper work thereof. To outvie the demerits of our sins was the perfection of his death, but to save our souls is the end and perfection of his intercession. Our sins are the object of the one, and our souls of the other. To that end was intercession added to his death, that we might not have a right to heaven in vain, of which we might be dispossessed. Now therefore, upon this ground, if Christ should fail of our souls' salvation, yea, but of any one degree of glory (purchased by his death to any soul) which that soul should want, this work of his would then want and fall short so much of its perfection. That place in Heb. 7 says not only that Christ will do his utmost to save, but save to the utmost.

Obj. You may say, My infidelity and obstinacy may hinder it, though Christ doth what in him lies.

Ans. Well, but intercession undertakes the work absolutely; for Christ prays not conditionally in heaven, 'If men shall believe, *etc.*', as we do here on earth; not for propositions only, but for persons; and therefore he prays to cure that very infidelity. Now, as if a physician undertakes to cure a madman (if he knows what he doth), he considers the madness of his patient, and how he will tear off what is applied, and refuse all physic; he therefore resolves to deal with him accordingly, and so to order him as he shall not hinder that help which he is about to afford him, and so upon those terms he undertakes the cure: even so doth Christ, when by intercession he undertakes to save us sinners; he considers us what we are, and how it is with us, what unbelief is in us, yet undertakes the matter; and so to save us is the scope and end of this his work, which if he should not accomplish, he after all this should not be a perfect priest. It was the fault that God found with the old priesthood, that it 'made nothing perfect', Heb. 7:19, and therefore, verse 12, the 'law was changed'; and the 'priesthood was changed' together with it, as there you have it.

Now in like manner Christ's priesthood should be imperfect, if it made not the elect perfect, and then God must yet seek for another covenant, and a more perfect priest; for this would be found faulty, as the other was. So then our comfort is, if Christ approve himself to be a perfect priest, we who come to God by him must be perfectly saved. It is in this office of his priesthood, and all the parts of it, as in his kingly office. The work of his kingly office is to subdue all enemies, to the last man, even fully to do the thing; and not only to have power, and to go about to do it: so as if there should be any one enemy left unsubdued, then Christ should not be a perfect king. The same holds in his priestly office also; he should not be a perfect priest, if but one soul of the elect, or those he intercedes for, were left unsaved. And this is indeed the top and highest consideration for our comfort in this argument, that intercession leaves us not till it hath actually and completely saved us; and this is it that makes the apostle put a further thing upon intercession here in the text, than upon that other, his 'sitting at God's right hand'. So as we are in this respect as sure of attaining unto the utmost glory of our salvation, as Christ to have the full honour of his priesthood. A man saved is more than justified; and Christ cannot reckon his work, nor himself a perfect

[Sect. 5]

priest, until we are saved. 'Who shall condemn? It is Christ that intercedes.'

(2.) Besides the consideration of the nature and scope of this work itself, which Christ, upon his honour of acquitting himself as a perfect priest, hath undertaken, there is in the second place a farther consideration that argues him engaged by a stronger obligation, even the loss of his own honour, his office, and all, if he should not effect salvation for those that come to God by him; so much doth it concern him to effect it. Of all the works that ever he did, he is most engaged in this; it will not only be the loss of a business which concerns him, and of so much work, but himself must be lost in it too; and the reason is, that he intercedes as a *Surety*. He was not only a 'surety on earth' in dying, and so was to look to do that work throughly, and to be sure to lay down a price sufficient, or else himself had gone for it: he pawned in that work, not only his honour, but even his life and soul to effect it, or lose himself in it; but he is a surety now also in heaven, by interceding. This you may find to be the scope of Heb. 7:22, by observing the coherence of that 22nd verse (wherein he is called a 'surety') with verses 23-25, that title and appellation is there given him, in relation unto this part of his office especially. And although it holds true of all parts of his office whatsoever, yet the coherence carries it, that that mention there of his being a surety doth in a more special manner refer unto his intercession, as appears both by the words before and after: in the words before, verse 21, the apostle speaks of this his 'priesthood, which is for ever', and then subjoins, verse 22, 'By so much was Jesus made a surety of a better testament'; and then after also he discourseth of, and instanceth in his intercession, and his continuing a priest for ever in that work: so, verse 23-25, 'Wherefore he is able to save to the utmost, seeing he ever lives to make intercession.' Yea, he is therefore engaged to save to the utmost, because even in interceding (for which he is said there to live) he is a surety.

He was a surety on earth, and is a surety still in heaven; only with this double difference, which ariseth first from the different things which he undertook for then, whilst on earth, and for which now he undertakes in heaven; that on earth he was a surety to pay a price so sufficient as should satisfy God's justice; which having paid, he was discharged (in that respect, and so far) of that obligation, and his bond for that was cancelled; but so as still he remains a surety, bound in another obligation as great, even for the bringing to salvation those whom he died for; for their persons remained still unsaved, though the debt was then paid; and till they be saved, he is not quit of this suretyship and engagement. And, secondly, these two suretyships do differ also by the differing pawns which he was engaged to forfeit, by failing in each of these works: for the payment of our debt, his soul itself lay at the stake, which he offered up for sin; but for the saving of the persons all his honour in heaven lies at stake. He lives to intercede. He possesseth heaven upon these terms, and it is one end of his life; so that as he must have sunk under God's wrath, if he had not paid the debt, his soul standing in our souls' stead, so he must yet quit heaven, and give over living there, if he brings us not thither. It is true, he intercedes not as a common person (which relation in all other forementioned acts he still bore; thus in his death he was both a common person and a surety representing us, so as we died in him; so likewise in his resurrection we arose with him, and in his ascension we ascended, *etc.*, but yet he intercedes not under that relation, namely, not as a common person), for we must not, cannot be said to intercede in him, for this last work lay not upon us to do. He doth it wholly for us indeed, but not in our stead, or as that which we should have done, though on our behalf; for it being the last, the crown of all his works of mediation, is therefore proper to him as Mediator, and his sole work as such. Thus in like manner the first work of incarnation, and answerably the last of intercession, in neither of these was Christ a common person representing others, though a common Saviour of others in these. For the one was the foundation of all, the other the accomplishment of all, and so proper only to himself as mediator. But although he intercedes not as a common person, as representing us in what we were to have done for ourselves; yet, so as that other relation of a surety is continued still in that work, he stands engaged therein as an undertaker for us, and so as a surety intercedes: such as Judah was for Benjamin, Gen. 43:9, 'I will be surety for him; of my hand shalt thou require him: if I bring him not unto thee, and set him before thee, then let me bear the blame for ever.' So says Christ for us. And therefore *sponsio*, or undertaking for us, is by divines made a great part of this part of his office. Now the consideration of this may the more secure us; for the more peculiarly and solely it is his work, the more his honour lies at stake, and the more he will set himself to effect it; yea, and being by way of suretyship, it concerns him yet more nearly, for he hath engaged, and if he should fail, might even lose that honour which he hath now in heaven.

[Sect. 5]

Chapter 5

*The prevalency of Christ's intercession, and the powerful
influence it hath into our salvation, demonstrated, first,
from the greatness of Christ, and his favour with God.*

2. Thus we have heard what matter of support to
our faith, by way of evidence, this must needs afford,
that Christ intercedes. Let us consider now what
further assurance will arise to our faith, from the
influence which Christ's intercession must needs have,
to effect and carry on our salvation to an assured
issue. The work of intercession being effectually to
procure our salvation, and to continue the pardon of
our sins, and hold us in favour with God, therefore
the influence and energy it hath herein must needs
lie in that potency and prevalency which this intercession of Christ hath with God, to obtain anything
at his hands for us, and so to continue his favour
towards us. Now, to raise up our apprehensions how
potent and prevalent this intercession of Christ must
needs be, let us consider both the *Person interceding*,
namely, Christ; and the *Person with whom* Christ
intercedes for this favour, which is God; the one
the Son, the other the Father; and so the greatness

of Christ with God, and the graciousness of God to Christ, together with the oneness of wills and unity of affections in them both: so that Christ will be sure to ask nothing which his Father will deny, and his Father will not deny anything which he shall ask.

(1.) Now, first, for the greatness of Christ the Intercessor, that is, his greatness with God the Father. This is often urged in this Epistle to the Hebrews, to persuade confidence in us, in this very point in hand; thus, Heb. 4:14, 16, 'Seeing we have a *great* high priest, let us come boldly.' And whilst *great* and *priest* are thus joined together, the more comfort and boldness we may have, the greater he is; for he is a priest in relation to his dealing with God for our pardon. As he is a priest, he deals in nothing else; and the greater the person is who useth his interest herein, the better, the sooner he will prevail. And he is there said to be *great*, because great with God, in prevailing with him; and indeed so great, as it is impossible but he should prevail. It was the greatness of his person which did and doth put such an influence into his death, that it was, as you heard, a price more than enough to satisfy justice, even to overflowing. And therefore, 'Who shall condemn? It is Christ that died.' And the greatness of his person must needs have as much influence to make intercession prevalent. In a matter of intercession, the person that intercedes prevails more than any other consideration whatsoever. We see what great friends do procure oftentimes with but a word speaking, even that which money, no, nor anything could have obtained. Now Christ must needs be great with God in many respects.

[1.] First, in respect of the nearness of his alliance to him. He is the natural Son of God, God of God, and therefore certain to prevail with him. This is diligently still put in, almost in all places, where this part of his priesthood (his intercession) is mentioned, in the Epistle to the Hebrews. So in chap. 4 of the same epistle, verse 14, 'We have a great high priest entered into the heavens, Jesus *the Son of God*.' So Heb. 7:25, and 28th verse compared, the apostle having said, verse 25, that 'he is able to save to the utmost, seeing he ever lives to make intercession', he doth, verse 28, devolve this ability of his to save (ultimately) upon his being the Son; thus in the 28th verse, in the end of that discourse, this is made as the basis of all: 'The law [saith he] makes men high priests which have infirmity', which infirmity or disability of theirs is mentioned in opposition unto what he had just before spoken of the great ability of this our high priest in his interceding, verse 25, in those words, 'He is able to save to the utmost.'

Those priests whom the ceremonial law made, Aaron and his sons, are unable to save, they have infirmity. Now what is it in him that makes this difference, and him so able above what they were? 'The word of the oath makes the *Son* [says he], who is perfected [as you have it in the Greek and margin] for evermore.' He mentions this his sonship principally in relation to his intercession, which there he had discoursed of. Intercession is a carrying on our salvation in a way of grace and favour, as his death was by way of satisfaction.

And answerably it may be observed in the Scripture, that as the all-sufficiency of the satisfaction of his death is still put upon his being God; and so upon the greatness of his person considered in respect of his nature or essence, namely, his Godhead; so in like manner, that the prevalency of his intercession is founded upon the nearness of his relation unto God, his alliance to him, and the being his Son. Thus for the first. When redemption is spoken of, the sufficiency of the price is eminently put upon his Godhead, 'the blood of God'. Thus also, Heb. 9, where when he had, verse 12, shown how Christ had purchased and obtained a 'perfect redemption', he then argues the sufficiency of it from his Godhead, verses 13, 14, 'For if the blood of bulls and of goats, and the ashes of an heifer sprinkling the unclean, sanctifieth to the purifying of the flesh; how much more shall the blood of Christ, who through the eternal Spirit offered himself?' *etc*. The eternal Spirit is his Godhead. Thus answerably, when he speaks of the prevailing of his intercession in heaven, he puts it upon his sonship; 'Jesus the Son'. He mentions the nearness of the relation of his person to God, as being that which draws with it that great respect, and favour, and grace, he being by this great with God, as great in himself. All matters of intercession are carried, we know, by way of favour. And therefore look how prevalent in a way of merit his being God makes his death in its kind; no less prevalent doth his being the Son of God make his intercession in its kind, namely, in a way of obtaining grace and mercy; yea, so prevalent of itself it is, that we might build upon it alone, even as much as upon his death. And, indeed, Christ intercedes not only in the virtue and strength of his satisfaction, though in that also, and of his obedience to his Father but also in the strength of his relation as a Son who pleads his own grace and interest in God, as he is his Son, which is a consideration that doth always actually exist and abide. Whereas his obedience, though perfect, was but once offered up, and its existence is but virtual; but he continues a Son for ever, not virtually only, but actually. And therefore it is added in that 7th to the Hebrews, verse 28, that the 'gospel ordained the Son, *perfected for ever*'. The meaning whereof is, that he is not only a priest, perfected in the time past by that perfect offering once made, but in that he is the Son, he remains a perfect priest for ever, for time to come; whom therefore no imperfection in his office, no failing or missing of his suits can befall. So as if it could be supposed that his obedience, because past so long ago, might be forgotten; yet never this, that he is a Son. That for ever abides, and of itself were enough to prevail. And how effectual must the intercession of such a Son be, who is so great a Son of so great a Father, equal with him, and the express image of his person? Never any Son so like, and in so peculiarly a transcendent manner a Son, as the relation of sonship among men is but a shadow of it! Christ is one with his Father, as himself often speaks; and, therefore, if his Father should deny him anything, he should then cease to be one with him, he must then 'deny himself', which God can never do. He is in this respect 'the Beloved', as he is called, Eph. 1:6, as on whom (originally and primarily) all the beams of God's love do fall. Solomon (the type of Christ) was 'the beloved of God', 2 Sam. 12:24, and had his name from thence (namely) *Jedidiah*, that is, 'beloved of the Lord'. And to show how beloved he was, God, when he came first into his kingdom, bade him 'ask what he should give him', 1 Kings 3:5. Now the like God says to Christ, when come first to his kingdom, also, Psa. 2:8, 'Ask of me, and I will give thee', namely, when 'he had set him as king on his holy hill', verse 6; and of him he says, 'This is my well-beloved Son, in whom I am well pleased, hear him.' God bids us therefore and upon that respect to hear him; and that speech was but the echo of his own heart, in that he himself is so well pleased with him for this that he is his Son, as he himself will hear him in everything; yea, and is so pleased with him, as that although Christ had never died nor obeyed the law, yet simply because he is his Son, he hath so full an acquiescency of all desires in him, and com-placency of delights, that he could deny him nothing. How prevalent then must Christ's intercession needs be, though there were nothing else to be considered!

And that God had indeed this as one main con-sideration upon which he made him a priest thus to intercede, those words do testify, Heb. 5:5, 6, 'He that said, unto him, Thou art my Son, this day have I begotten thee. As he saith also in another place, Thou art a priest for ever, after the order of Melchisedec.' These latter words are not only a paraphrase (as some think) merely to show that he that said, 'Christ was his Son', said also, 'he was a priest'; but it is to show the foundation of his call to that office. The great consideration that fitted him for it was, that he was God's Son; especially that fitted him for that part of his priesthood which was to remain 'for ever', of which that 110th Psalm and the Epistle to the Hebrews do especially speak. Neither is the meaning of the fore-cited place only to show that in that he was God's Son, it was his birthright to be a priest, so as if God would have any priest at all it must be he, and so, upon that consideration, he that said to him, 'Thou art my Son', said, 'Thou art a priest'; and that being his right, he therefore called him to it, because he was his Son, for, according to the law of nature, the eldest of the family was to be priest; and so Christ, even as God-man, being the 'first-born of every creature', and the natural first begotten Son of God, had right to be the prime leader of that great chorus in that eternal worship in heaven. That (I say) is not all the meaning of those words, nor all that God considered in it, when he thus ordained him to be a priest; but he had a further and more peculiar respect unto this especial part of his priesthood, his intercession (as that clause 'forever' imports), as for which, he being his natural Son, so nearly allied to him, would transcendently fit him, and give such an omnipotent prevalency and effectualness to his requests, that he would be the most absolute perfect priest for ever, in this respect, that could be.

That as God himself is perfect, and his power irresistible, so his priesthood, through this relation, might be perfect also, and his requests undeniable. Thus did God order it to strengthen our faith. And that, indeed, God did consider this relation of his to him to this very end, is evident by that of the 2nd Psalm, out of which that saying, 'Thou art my Son', is cited, verses 7 and 8, 'Thou art my Son, this day have I begotten thee'; and what follows? 'Ask of me, and I will give thee', *etc.* He connects both these together, namely, intercession, that part of his priestly office of asking, with his sonship, for that is it which moveth God to grant all that he asks. God loves Christ as he loves himself, and therefore can deny him nothing, as he cannot deny himself. And so, by the way, this clears the ground of the apostle's quoting those words of Psa. 2 in Heb. 5, as a proof of Christ's call to the priesthood, which interpreters have been troubled how to make out; for (as you have seen) that speech, 'Thou art my Son, ask', *etc.*, is all one as if he had said, 'Thou art a priest'; and so was as fit and full a place to prove his being a priest in the Holy Ghost's intent, as is that other quoted with it, out of Psa. 110, though uttered in more express words, 'Thou art a priest for ever.' Both speeches come to one in both places, the Holy Ghost especially aiming in both at that part of his priesthood in heaven, his intercession: in the one speaking of him after he is set upon God's hill as king (so Psa. 2:6); and in the other, after he is set down at God's right hand (so Psa. 110:1, 2). Yea, and this his favour with his Father, and intercession alone, might have procured pardon for us sinners, but that God's will was to have justice satisfied.

[2.] And secondly, he intercedes not only as a Son (and in that respect a priest perfect enough for ever), but also as a Son who hath been obedient to his Father, and hath done at his request, and for his sake, the greatest service for him, and the most willingly that ever was done. And you all know how much former services done do always forward suits. In Heb. 5, verses 8-10, it is said, that 'though he were a Son, yet learned he obedience', and thereby 'became perfect'. The apostle had said, in the verses before, that in respect of his being his Son, God had called him to this office, as one that was thereby sufficiently qualified to be a priest that might prevail: and yet in these verses he further adds, that though he was a Son, and in that respect a priest perfect enough, yet he was to be obedient also, and thereby yet to become, in a further respect, a perfect high priest also, even in respect of service done and obedience performed. And so shows that he comes to have a further perfection and power of prevailing in his priestly office added to that relation of sonship spoken of, verse 5. And therefore it follows, that he being thus become perfect, namely, through his obedience, 'he became author of eternal salvation unto all them that obey him, called of God an high priest for ever', *etc.* That therefore which makes him yet more potent, that he may be sure to prevail, is his obedience and service done; and this alone also were enough to carry anything. And both these considerations, of his sonship and obedience, as giving an efficacy to his intercession, you have also in that, Heb. 7. From verse 26 to 28, he had spoken of the power of intercession, verses 24, 25, how he was 'able to save to the utmost'; and then, in the following verse, he shows the ground of it, first in his fore-past 'obedience', verse 26. *First, active,* 'for such a high priest became us, who was holy, harmless, undefiled'. And such a priest he was, and therefore able thus to save by his intercession. For such an one who was holy, harmless, and no guile found in his mouth, what requests come out of such lips must needs be accepted. Then, secondly, he mentions his *passive obedience*, verse 27, 'He offered up himself once', and thereby made so full a satisfaction, as he needed not to do it but once; and in the strength of both these he intercedes, for to that purpose doth the mention of both these there come in. And then he adds that other which we before insisted on, that he is the Son, which follows in the next words, verse 28. And accordingly you shall find Christ himself urging this his obedience, as the foundation of all those his suits and requests for us that follow after. So in that last prayer, John 17 (which is, as it were, a pattern or instance of his intercession for us in heaven), 'I have glorified thee on earth, I have finished the work thou gavest me', verse 4. And whereas two things may be distinctly considered, in that his obedience. First, the worth of it, as a price in the valuation of justice itself; secondly, the desert of favour and grace with God; which such an obedience and service, done for his sake, might in a way of kindness expect to find at his hands. You may for your comfort consider, that besides what the worth of it as a price, which I shall urge in the next chapter, might exact of justice itself between two strangers (as we use to say), he having well paid for all that he asks; he hath, moreover, deserved thus much grace and favour with his Father, in that this obedience was done for his sake and at his request; and this it calls for even in way of remuneration and requital, as of one kindness with the like. That therefore his Father should hear him in all the requests that ever he should make, yea so transcendent was the obedience which he did to his Father, in giving himself to death at his request (and it was done at God's sole entreaty, 'Lo! I come to do thy will'), as he can never out-ask the merit of this his service. And, which may yet further encourage us herein, he hath nothing at all left to ask for himself simply, for he hath need of nothing. So that all his favour remains entire, for to be laid forth for sinners, and employed for them. And then add this thereto, that all he can ask for them is less, yea far less, than the service which he hath done to God comes to; our lives, and pardon, and salvation, these are not enough, they are too small a requital. So that besides his natural grace and interest which he hath with his Father, as he is his Son, which can never be lessened, this his acquired favour by his obedience must needs make him prevail, seeing it can never be acquitted to the full. Some divines put so much efficacy in this, that they say, Christ's very being in heaven, who once did this service, and so putting God in mind of it by his very presence, is all that intercession that the Scripture speaks of; so sufficient they think this alone to be.

Chapter 6

Secondly, the prevalency of Christ's intercession demon-strated from the righteousness of the cause he pleads even in justice; how forcible the cry of his blood is, himself appearing to intercede with it.

Besides favour and grace in all these respects, he can and doth plead justice and righteousness, and is able so to carry it; so you have it, 1 John 2:1 and 2, 'We have an advocate with the Father, Jesus Christ *the righteous.*' An advocate hath place only in a cause of justice, and this Christ's advocateship is executed by pleading his own satisfaction. So it follows, 'who is a propitiation for our sins'; and can plead his own righteousness so far, that justice itself shall be fain to save the worst of sinners. He can turn justice itself for them, and handle matters so, as justice shall be as forward to save them as any other attribute. So that if God be said to be 'righteous in forgiving us our sins, if we do but confess them' (as chap. 1 of this First Epistle of John, verse 9), then much more when 'Jesus Christ the righteous' shall intercede for the pardon of them, as he adds in the 2nd verse of the ensuing chapter, and this if he will be just. The worst case he will make a good one; not with colouring it over, as cunning lawyers do, or extenuating things; but with pleading that righteousness, which being put into the opposite balance, shall cast it for thee, be there never so many sins weighed against it. Yea, and he will be just in it too, and carry all by mere righteousness and equity.

In the explication of this branch, my purpose is not to insist upon the demonstration of that all-sufficient fulness that is in Christ's satisfaction, such as may in justice procure our pardon and salvation (because it will more fitly belong to another discourse), but I shall absolve this point in hand by two things which are proper to this head of intercession.

[1.] First, by showing how that there is even in respect to God's justice a powerful voice of intercession attributed unto Christ's blood; and how prevalent that must needs be in the ears of the righteous God.

[2.] Secondly, especially when Christ himself shall join with that cry and intercession of his blood, himself in heaven appearing and interceding in the strength of it.

[1.] For the first, the apostle, Heb. 12:24, doth ascribe a voice, an appeal, an intercession unto the blood of Christ in heaven. 'The blood of sprinkling' (says he) 'speaks better things than the blood of Abel.' He makes Christ's very blood an advocate to speak for us, though Christ himself were silent, as he says in another case, 'Abel, though dead, yet speaketh', Heb. 11:4. Many other things are said to cry in Scripture (and I might show how the cry of all other things do meet in this), but blood hath the loudest cry of all things else, in the ears of the Lord of Hosts, the Judge of all the world, as he is in the 23rd verse of that 12th chapter styled. Neither hath any cry the ear of God's justice more than that of blood. 'The voice of thy brother's blood', says God to Cain, 'cries unto me from the ground', Gen. 4:10. Now in that speech of the apostle fore-cited, is the allusion made unto the blood of Abel, and the cry thereof. And he illustrates the cry of Christ's blood for us, by the cry of that blood of Abel against Cain, it 'speaks better things than the blood of Abel'. And his scope therein is by an *antithesis*, or way of opposition, to show that Christ's blood calls for greater *good* things to be bestowed on us *for whom* it was shed, than Abel's blood did for *evil* things, and vengeance against Cain, *by whom* it was shed. For look how loud the blood of one innocent cries for justice against another that murdered him; so loud will the blood of one right-eous, who by the appointment and permission of a supreme judge hath been condemned for another, cry for his release and non-condemnation, for whom he died. And the more righteous he was, who laid down his life for another, the louder still is that cry, for it is made in the strength of all that worth which was in him, whose blood was shed. Now to set forth the power of this cry of Christ's blood with justice, let us compare it with that cry of Abel's blood in these two things, wherein it will be found infinitely to exceed it in force and loudness.

First, even the blood of the wickedest man on earth, if innocently shed, doth cry, and hath a power with justice against him who murdered him. Had Abel murdered Cain, Cain's blood would have cried, and called upon God's justice against Abel; but Abel's blood (there is an emphasis in that), Abel's, who was a saint, and the first martyr in God's calendar; and so his blood cries according to the worth that was in him. Now 'precious in the sight of the Lord is the death of his saints'; and the blood of one of them cries louder than the blood of all mankind besides. Now from this I argue, if the blood of a saint cries so, what must the blood of the King of saints (as Christ is called, Rev. 15:3), then do? If the blood of one member of Christ's body, what will then the blood of the head, far more worth than that whole body?

How doth it fill heaven and earth with outcries, until the promised intent of its shedding be accomplished! And (as the antithesis carries it) look how the blood of Abel cried for the ruin and condemnation of his brother Cain; so does Christ's blood on the contrary for our pardon and non-condemnation; and so much louder, by how much his blood was of more worth than Abel's was. This was the 'blood of God'; so Acts 20:28, 'Who therefore shall condemn?' But,

Secondly, Christ's blood hath in its cry here a further advantage of Abel's blood attributed to it. For that cried but from earth, 'from the ground', where it lay shed, and that but for an answerable earthly punishment on Cain, as he was a man upon the earth; but Christ's blood is carried up to heaven; for as the high priest carried the blood of the sacrifices into the holy of holies, so hath Christ virtually carried his blood into heaven, Heb. 9:12. And this is intimated in this place also, as by the coherence will appear. For all the other particulars (of which this is one), whereto he says the saints are come, they are all in heaven. 'You are come [says he, verse 22] to the city of the living God, the heavenly Jerusalem, and to an innumerable company of angels, to the church of the first-born who are written in heaven, and to God the judge of all, and to the spirits of just men made perfect.' All which things are in heaven; neither names he any other than such; and then adds, 'and to the blood of sprinkling, which speaks', *etc.*, as a thing both speaking in heaven, and besprinkled from heaven, yea, wherewith heaven is all besprinkled, as the mercy-seat in the holy of holies was, because sinners are to come thither. This blood therefore cries from heaven, it is next unto God who sits judge there, it cries in his very ears; whereas the cry of blood from the ground is further off, and so though the cry thereof may come up to heaven, yet the blood itself comes not up thither, as Christ already is. Abel's blood cried for vengeance to come down from heaven, but Christ's blood cries us up into heaven; like to that voice, Rev. 11:12, 'Come up hither.' So John 17:24, 'Where I am, let them be' for whom this blood was shed.

But though this speaking, this voice and intercession, be attributed to his blood, yet it is but in a metaphorical and improper (though real) sense; as also that this blood is in heaven, is spoken, though in a real, yet not a proper sense. Some divines of all sides, both popish and protestant, would make the whole work of intercession to be only metaphorical. It is true indeed, the voice and intercession of his blood apart considered, is but metaphorical (I grant), and yet real; such a voice as those groans are that are attributed to the whole creation, Rom. 8:22. But intercession as an act of Christ himself, joined with this voice of his blood, is most properly and truly such.

[2.] Therefore, in the second place, add to this Christ's own intercession also, which was the second thing propounded, that Christ by his own prayers seconds this cry of his blood; that not only the blood of Christ doth cry, but that Christ himself being alive doth join with it. How forcible and prevalent must all this be supposed to be! The blood of a man slain doth cry, though the man remain dead; even as of Abel, it is said (though to another purpose), that 'being dead he yet speaketh', Heb. 11, but Christ liveth and appeareth, *Vivit, et in cœlum cœlorum venit.*[1] He follows the suit, pursues the hue and cry of his blood himself. His being alive, puts a life into his death. It is not in this as it was in that other, the first Adam's sin and disobedience. Adam, although he himself had been annihilated when he died, yet he having set the stock of our nature a-going in propagation of children, his sin would have defiled and condemned them to the end of the world, and the force of it to condemn is neither furthered nor

---

[1] Latin: He lives, and enters the heaven of heavens. — P.

lessened by his subsisting and being, or his not being; it receives no assistance from his personal life, one way or other. And the reason is, because his sin condemns us in a natural and necessary way; but the death of Christ and his blood shed, these saving us in a way of grace and favour unto Christ himself and for his sake, that very being alive of Christ, that shed this blood, adds an infinite acceptation to it with God, and moves him the more to hear the cry of it, and to regard it. In a matter of favour to be done for the sake of another man, or in a suit or matter of justice that concerns another who is interested in it, that man's being *in vivis*, his being alive, puts a life into the cause. If David would have respect to Jonathan (when dead) in his children, he would much more if himself had been alive. God made a covenant with Abraham, Isaac, and Jacob, to remember their seed after them; and why? They are alive, and were to live for ever; and though dead, shall rise again. So Christ reasoneth from it, Matt. 22:32, 'I am the God of Abraham, Isaac, and Jacob. God is the God of the living (says he), and not of the dead'; and so, 'though Abraham be ignorant of his children' (as the prophet speaks) and should not intercede for them, yet because Abraham's soul lives, and is not extinct (as the Sadducees thought), but shall live again at the resurrection, therefore God remembers and respects his covenant with them; for he is a God of the living, and so his covenant holds with them whilst they live. The old covenant of the first Testament ran in the names of Abraham, Isaac, and Jacob—'the God of Abraham, Isaac, and Jacob'—but this new covenant runs in the name of Christ, 'The God and Father of our Lord Jesus Christ'; so Eph. 1:3, and so he becomes our God and our Father in him. And God being thus our Father, because Christ's Father, and Christ (in whose name the covenant runs) being alive, and God by covenant the God of a living, not of a dead Christ, this therefore works effectually with him to respect his blood and hear the cry of it; and this, though Christ were absent, much more then when he is present also, and on purpose 'appeareth in the presence of God for us'; as it is, Heb. 9:24. He is alive, and so able to follow his own suit, and will be sure to see to it, and to second the cry of his blood, if it should not be heard.

To illustrate this by the help of the former comparison begun. If as Abel's blood cries, so also it proves that Abel's soul lives to cry; that both his cause cries and himself lives to follow it; so that the cry of Abel's blood is seconded with the cry of Abel's soul that lives, how doubly forcible must this needs be? And thus indeed you have it, Rev. 6:9, where it is said that 'the souls of them which were slain for the testimony which they held, cried with a loud voice, saying, How long, Lord, holy and true, dost thou not avenge our blood?' Yea, see that not only their blood cries, but their souls live, and live to cry. And it is not spoken metaphorically of their souls, but what is truly done by them now in heaven, it being mentioned to show how and by what God was moved to bring vengeance on the heathenish empire of Rome that had shed their blood. Now not only Christ's soul (as theirs) lives to cry, but his whole person; for he is risen again, and lives to intercede for ever. In the Rev. 1, verse 18, Christ appearing to John, when he would speak but one speech that should move all in him, he says but this, 'I am he that liveth, and was dead', and died for thee. And whose heart doth it not move to read it with faith? And doth it not move his Father, think you, who was the chief cause and motioner of his death, to think, *my Son* that was dead, and died at my request for sinners, is now alive again, and liveth to intercede, and liveth to 'see the travail of his soul' fulfilled and satisfied? God pronounceth this upon it in that 53rd of Isaiah, verse 11, 'By his knowledge (or faith in him) shall he justify many'; even as many as he died for. 'Who then shall condemn? Christ that was dead is alive, and liveth to intercede.'

Chapter 7

Thirdly, the prevalency of Christ's intercession, and of his grace with his Father, demonstrated from the greatness and absoluteness of his power to do whatever he asks.

[3.] A third demonstration both of Christ's greatness with God, and his power to prevail for us, is taken from this, that God hath put all power into his hand, to do whatever he will, hath made him his king to do what pleaseth him either in heaven, earth, or hell; yea, to do all that God himself ever means to do, or all that God desires to do. And certainly if his Father hath been so gracious to him as to bestow so high and absolute a sovereignty on him, as to accomplish and effect whatever he means to do, surely his purpose was never to deny Christ any request that he should after this make: he would never have advanced the human nature to that absoluteness else. Those two great monarchs made great grants and largesses, the one to Esther, the other to Herodias's daughter; but yet they were limited only to the half of their kingdoms; so Mark 6:22. and Esth. 5:6, and the royal power in their kingdoms they meant still to retain and reserve wholly to themselves. But God having placed Christ on his throne, bids him ask even to the whole of his kingdom, for God hath made him a king, sitting on his throne with him, not to share halves, but to have all power in heaven and earth; 'he hath committed all judgment to the Son', to save and condemn whomever he will; and so far as the kingdom of God goes, or is extended, he may do anything. So John 5:21, 'As the Father raiseth up the dead, so the Son quickeneth whom he will; for as the Father hath life in himself, so hath he given to the Son to have life in himself', verse 26; and hath in like manner 'given authority to execute judgment also, as the Son of man' (namely, of himself), verse 27; as he said, 'he had given him to have life in himself', verse 26, not dependently, as we have, but independently, so to execute judgment also, verse 27. So that Christ's will is as free, and himself as absolute a monarch and king of himself, as God himself is. He indeed hath it not *a se ipso*, but *in se ipso*; not *a se ipso* originally, but from his Father; but *in se ipso*, independently.[1]

Now, then, if he who is king, and may and doth of himself command all that is done, as absolutely as

---

[1] Latin: *a se ipso*: from himself; *in se ipso*: in himself. —P.

God himself doth, I speak in respect of the execution of things downward, by second causes; if he, over and above, to honour his Father, will ask all that himself hath power to do, what will not be done? *Qui rogat, et imperare potest*;[1] he that can and doth command whatever he would have done, and it is straight done, if he shall ask and entreat, what will not be done? As a king who sues for peace, backed with a potent army which is able to win what he entreats for, must needs treat more effectually, so doth Christ sue for everything with power to effect it. Remember that he is said here in the text, first to be at God's right hand, and there to intercede. He treats the salvation of sinners as a mighty prince treats the giving up some town to him, which lies seated under a castle of his which commands that town: he stands treating with the governor, having his ordnance ready for the battery, and to bring all into subjection, as 2 Cor. 10:4. And this is a consideration that God himself took, in that 2nd Psalm, when he made him that promise, 'Ask, and I will give thee', why he made so large a grant. He had said before, verse 6, 'I have set my king upon my holy hill of Sion', which made him, one would think, past asking, and above the condition of an intercessor. Now God says of him, 'He

---

[1] Latin: The one who asks also has power to command. —P.

is my king', not in respect of his commanding God (that were blasphemy to think), but it is spoken in respect of commanding all below him. God having set him in his throne, to do as much as he himself would, or means to have done, says, he is my king, to rule all, not so much under me as for me, and in my stead, yet absolutely, and in himself; 'the Father judgeth no man'. Now when the Father had first made and constituted him thus great a king, then he bids him ask, to whom he had first given this absolute power to command. We may, without blasphemy, say of this God-man, that God hath not only not the heart, as being his Father, but not the power to cross anything he doth. Thus fast hath he God unto him. Only he who in respect of this his power is to be honoured as the Father, as John 5:23, yet to honour his Father, who gave this power originally to him as mediator, he is to ask for that which of himself he yet can do. And therefore, says God, though thou art a king (so verse 6), and all my kingdom, even 'the utmost ends of the earth', are 'thine inheritance' by a natural right, now that thou art my Son (as verse 8); yet because thou art my king, of my appointing, and 'I have set thee' on the throne (as the word is, verse 6), and 'thou art my Son, and I have begotten thee', therefore acknowledge my grant in all, 'ask of me, and I will give thee the utmost ends of the earth for thy inheritance'. I cannot deny thee, but I would have thee ask; and therefore Christ asks. Yet still withal remember, that he asks who can command the thing to be done; and yet, as he must ask ere the thing be done, so if he ask it must needs be granted. These are the terms between this Father and this Son, who, in a word, had not been so great a Father if he had not had a Son thus great, that himself could not deny what this Son would have done. It is for his own honour to have such a Son: so John 5:23, 'That they might honour the Son as they honour the Father', therefore 'all judgment is committed to him'. Now, then, if he who hath so much power will join the force of entreaty with a Father that so loves him; if he who is the word of his Father, that commands, creates, and upholds all, as Heb. 1, 'He spake, and it was done'; if he will become a word to his Father, and speak a word for us, and ask all that he means to do; how forcible will such words be!

Therefore, observe Christ's manner of praying, John 17 (which prayer is a platform of intercession in heaven), verse 24, 'Father, *I will* that they whom thou hast given me be where I am.' He prays like a king, who is in joint commission with God. If God puts that honour upon our prayers, that we are said 'to have power with God', as Jacob, Hos. 12:3, that if God be never so angry, yet by 'taking hold of his strength', we hold his hands, as Isa. 27:5, that God cries out to Moses, like a man whose hands are held, 'Let me alone', Exod. 32:10, yea that he accounts it as a command and a *mandamus*,[1] so he styles it, Isa. 45:11, 'command ye me', so unable is he to go against it; then, how much more doth Jesus Christ's intercession bind God's hands, and command all in heaven and earth! Therefore, Zech. 1:12, you have Christ, 'the Angel of the covenant', brought in interceding with the Father for his church; and he speaks abruptly as one full of complaints, and in an expostulating way, 'Lord of Hosts, how long wilt thou not be merciful to Jerusalem and the cities of Judah?' and, verse 13, Zechariah saith, that he observed that 'the Lord answered the Angel with good words and comfortable'. God was fain to give him good words (as we use to say), that is, words that might pacify him, as words of comfort to us, so good words in respect to the Angel's complaint. And you may observe, how in the answer God returns upon it (which he bade Zechariah write), God excuseth it, as it were, to Christ, that his church had been

---

[1] Latin: lit. we command. Used in English to denote a directive from a superior to an inferior court.—P.

so long and so hardly dealt withal; as if beyond his intention, he lays the fault on the instruments, 'I was but a little displeased, but they helped forward the affliction', verse 15. This is spoken and carried after the manner of men, to show how tender God is of displeasing Christ our intercessor: that when Christ hath, as it were, been a long while silent, and let God alone, and his people have been ill dealt withal, he on the sudden in the end intercedes and complains of it, and it is not only instantly redressed, but excused for times past, with 'good words, and comfortable words'. Christ's Father will not displease him, nor go against him in anything.

Now that you may see a reason of this, and have all cavils and exceptions taken away, that may arise against this, and how that there is an impossibility that it should be otherwise, know that this Father and this Son, though two persons, have yet but one will between them, and but one power between them (though the Son, *ad extra*, outwardly executes all). John 10:30, 'My Father and I are one'; that is, have but one and the same power to save you, and one mind and will. So also, John 5:19, 'The Son can do nothing of himself, but what he sees the Father do; and whatever he doth, the same the Father doth also': they conspire in one, have one power, one will; and then it is no matter though God commit all power to the Son, and that the Son, though he hath all power, must ask all of the Father, for to be sure whatever he asks, the Father hath not power to deny, for they have but one will and power. They are one; so as if God deny him, he must deny himself, which the apostle tells us he cannot do, 2 Tim. 2:13. And so in the same sense that God is said not to have power to deny himself, in the same sense it may be said, he hath not power to deny Christ what he asks. Therefore God might well make him an absolute king, and betrust him with all power; and Christ might well oblige himself, notwithstanding this power, to ask all that he means to do; for they have but one will and one power, so as our salvation is made sure by this on all hands. 'I come not to do my will, but the will of him who sent me; and his will is, that I should lose none of all those whom he hath given me', John 6:38, 39. And therefore, 'who shall condemn? It is Christ that intercedes.' As who shall resist God's will? (as the apostle speaks) so who shall resist or gainsay Christ's intercession? God himself cannot, no more than he can gainsay or deny himself.

Chapter 8

The potency and prevalency of Christ's intercession, dem-
onstrated from the graciousness of the person with
whom he intercedes, considered first as he is the Father
of Christ himself.

(2.) We have seen the greatness of the person interceding, and many considerations from thence, which may persuade us of his prevailing for us. Let us now, in the next place, consider the graciousness of the person with whom he intercedes, which the Scripture, for our comfort herein, doth distinctly set before us, to the end that in this great matter our joy and security may every way be full. Thus in that, 1 John 2:1, when for the comfort and support of believers, against the evil of the greatest sins that can befall them after conversion, the apostle minds them of Christ's intercession in those words, 'If any man sin, we have an advocate, Jesus Christ the righteous'; mentioning therein the power and prevalency of such an advocate, through his own righteousness. But yet, over and above all this, the more fully to assure us of his good success herein for us, he also adds, 'An advocate *with the Father*.' He insinuates and suggests the relation and gracious disposition of him upon whose supreme will our case ultimately dependeth, 'the Father', as affording a new comfort and encouragement, even as great as doth the righteousness and power of the person interceding. He says not, 'with God' only, as elsewhere, but 'with the Father'. And that his words might afford the more full matter of confidence, and be the more comprehensive, and take in all, he expresseth not this relation of God limitedly, as confined to his Fatherhood, either unto Christ only, or us alone. He says not only, 'an advocate with *his* Father', though that would have given much assurance, or 'with *your* Father', though that might afford much boldness; but indefinitely he says, 'with *the* Father', as intending to take in both; to ascertain us of the prevailing efficacy of Christ's intercession from both. You have both these elsewhere more distinctly, and on purpose, and together mentioned, John 20:17, 'I go to my Father, and your Father', says Christ there. And it was spoken after that all his disciples had before forsaken him, and Peter denied him; when Christ himself could send them the greatest cordial that his heart could utter, and wrap up the strongest sublimation of comforts in one pill. What was it? Go, tell them (says he) not so much that I have satisfied for sin, overcome death, or am risen, but that 'I ascend'. For in that which Christ doth for us being ascended, lies the height, the top of our comfort. And whereas he might have said (and it had been matter of unspeakable comfort) I ascend to heaven, and so, where I am you shall be also; yet he chooseth rather to say, 'I ascend to the Father': for that indeed contained the foundation, spring, and cause of their comfort, even that relation of God's, his Fatherhood, with which Christ was to deal after his ascending for them. And because when, before his death, he had spoken of his going to his Father, their hearts had been troubled, John 14:28, they thinking it was for his own preferment only (as Christ's speech there implies they did) therefore he here distinctly adds, 'I ascend to my Father and your Father, to my God and your God.' He had in effect spoken as much before, in the words foregoing, 'Go, tell my brethren', but that was only implicitly; therefore, more plainly and explicitly he says it, for their further comfort, 'I go to my Father and your Father.' And consider that Christ being now newly risen, and having as yet not seen his disciples, and being now to send a message, his first message, a gospel of good tidings to them, and that in a brief sentence, by a woman; he chooseth out this as the first word to be spoken from him now, when he was come out of the other world, at their first hearsay of his return, he utters forth at once, the bottom, the depth, of all comfort, the sum of all joy, than which the gospel knows no greater, nor can go higher. So as if Christ should intend now at this day to send good news from heaven to any of you, it would be but this, I am here an advocate, interceding with my Father and thy Father. All is spoken in that. Even he could not speak more comfort, who is the God of comfort. Now, therefore, let us apart consider these two relations, which afford each of them their proper comfort and assurance; both that Christ is ascended and intercedes with *his own* Father, and also with *our* Father; and, therefore, how prevailing must this intercession be!

First, Christ intercedes with his Father, who neither will nor can deny him anything. To confirm this, you have a double testimony, and of two of the greatest witnesses in heaven: both a testimony of Christ's own, whilst he was on earth, and God's own word also declared since Christ came to heaven. The *former*, in the 11th of John, whilst Christ was here on earth, and had not as then fully performed that great service which he was to finish; which since he having done, it must needs ingratiate him the more with God his Father. When Lazarus was now four days dead, Martha, to move Christ to pity her, first tells him that if he had been there before her brother died, that then he had not died; and then (as having spoke too little) she adds, yea, thou canst, if thou pleasest, remedy it yet. 'But I know' (says she, verse 22) 'that even now' (though he be so long dead), 'whatever thou wilt ask of God, God will give it thee.' Here was her confidence in Christ's intercession, though this were a greater work than ever yet Christ had done any. And Christ seeing her faith in this, he confirms her speech when he came to raise him, and takes a solemn occasion to declare that God had never denied him any request that he had ever put up to him, first thanking God particularly that he had heard him in this, verse 41, 'Father, I thank thee that thou hast heard me.' He had (it seems) prayed for the thing at her entreaty; and now, before the thing was done, he (being assured his prayer was heard) gives thanks, so confident was he of his being heard. And then, secondly, shows upon what this his confidence at this time was grounded, his constant experience that God had never denied him any request; for it follows, verse 42, 'And I know that thou hearest me always', and therefore was so bold as to express my confidence in this before the thing was done, 'but because of them who stood by, I said it.' As if he had said, though I gave this public thanks for being heard only in this one miracle, and at no time the like so publicly; yet this is no new thing, but thus it hath been always hitherto in all the miracles I have wrought, and requests I have put up, which made me so to give thanks beforehand; and this is not the first time that God hath heard me thus, which I speak, that they might believe. Thus he was never denied on earth from the first to the last. For this was one of his greatest miracles, and reserved unto the last, even a few days before his crucifying.

And now he hath performed the service designed him, and is come to heaven, let us, *secondly*, hear God himself speak, what he means to do for him. You heard before, when he came first to heaven, what God said to him, and how he welcomed him with a 'Sit thou on my right hand till I make thine enemies thy footstool.' And before Christ opened his mouth to speak a word, by way of any request to God, which was the office that he was now to execute, God himself prevented him, and added, 'Thou art my Son; this day have I begotten thee. Ask of me, and I will give thee', Psa. 2:7, 8. He speaks it at Christ's first coming up to heaven, when he had his 'king on his holy hill', as verse 6. Christ was new glorified, which was as a new begetting to him, 'Today have I begotten thee.' And this is as if he had said, I know you will ask me now for all that you have died for: and this I promise you beforehand, before you speak a word, or make any request unto me, you shall ask nothing but it shall be granted; and this I speak once for all as a boon and a grace granted you upon your birthday, as the solemnest celebration of it; for such was his resurrection, and ascension, and sitting at God's right hand, 'This day have I begotten thee. Ask of me, and I will give thee.' So full of joy was his Father's heart that he had his Son in heaven with him, whom he had begotten from everlasting, and ordained to this glory, who was lately dead, and in a manner lost, and therefore now (as it were) new begotten. God's heart was so full that he could not hold from expressing it in the largest favours and grants. And whereas kings upon their own birthdays use to grant such favours to their favourites, so Herod on his birthday, to the daughter of Herodias, promised with an oath to give her whatsoever she would ask, Matt. 14:7. God himself having no birthday, not being of himself capable of it, yet having a Son who had, he honours him with that grace upon that day. And if Queen Esther (a subject, yea, a slave, in her original condition) was so prevalent for the Jews, her people and nation, when their case was desperate, and when there was an irrevocable decree past, and that not to be altered, for their ruin and destruction, then what will not Christ, so great a Son, even equal with his Father, prevail for with his Father for his brethren? Be their case for the time past never so desperate, be there never so many threatenings gone out against them, never so many precedents and examples of men condemned before for the like sins, and in the like case, yet Christ can prevail against them all.

Chapter 9

The potency of Christ's intercession demonstrated, in that he intercedes with God, who is our Father. — How God's heart is as much inclined to hear Christ for us as Christ's is to intercede.

Secondly, Christ is an advocate for us with our Father. You may perhaps think there is little in that, but Christ puts much upon it; yea, so much, as if that God would however grant all that Christ himself means to ask, whether Christ asked it or no. This you have expressly in John 16:26, 27, 'At that day (says Christ) you shall ask in my name: and I say not to you, that I will pray the Father for you: for the

Father himself loveth you.' To open this place, where he says 'at that day'. The day he means through this whole chapter, is that time when the Holy Ghost should be shed upon them; for throughout his discourse he still speaks of the fruits of his ascension, and of giving the Comforter, which was done upon his ascending, and was the first fruits of his priestly office in heaven. Thus Peter informs us, Acts 2:33, 'He being [says he] exalted by the right hand of God, and having received' (namely, by asking, 'Ask, and I will give thee') 'of the Father the promise of the Holy Ghost, he hath shed forth this, which you now see and hear.' Now, of that time when he shall be in heaven, he says, 'I say not that I will pray for you'; which is not meant that Christ prays not for us in heaven, but rather those very words are the highest intimation that he would and doth pray for us that can be. When men would most strongly intimate their purpose of a kindness they mean to do for one, they use to say, I do not say that I love you, or that I will do this or that for you; which is as much as to say, I will surely do it, and do it to purpose; but Christ's scope here is, as in the highest manner to promise them that he would pray for them; so withal, further to tell them of their more abundant assurance and security, that besides their having the benefit of their prayers, God himself so loves them of himself, that indeed that alone were enough to obtain anything at his hands, which they shall but ask in his name; so as he needs not pray for them, and yet he will too. But now in case that he himself pray for them, and they themselves in his name, and both unto a Father who of himself loveth them, and who hath purposed to grant all, before either he or they should ask; what hope must there needs be then of a good success! This is both the meaning of this place, and a great truth to be considered on by us, to the purpose in hand. That it is the meaning of the place, the manner of Christ's speech implies, 'I say not that I will pray the Father for you, for the Father himself loveth you.' It is such a speech as Christ used upon a clean contrary occasion, John 5:45, 'Do not think [says he] that I will accuse you to the Father: there is one who accuseth you, even Moses', *etc.* He there threatens the obstinate and accursed Pharisees with condemnation. Never stand thinking that it is I (says he) who am your only enemy and accuser, that will procure your condemnation, and so prosecute the matter against you merely for my own interest, no, I shall not need to do it; though I should not accuse you, your own 'Moses in whom you trust', he is enough to condemn you, he will do your errand sufficiently, you would be sure to be damned by his words and sayings; I shall not need to trouble myself to come in and enter my action against you too, Moses and his law would follow the suit, and be enough to condemn you to hell. So as this speech doth not imply that Christ will not at all accuse them; no, he means to bring in his action against them too; for he after says, if he had not spoke to them, they had had no sin, and therefore he meant to bring the greatest accusation of all. Now, in an opposite (though parallel) speech here, to comfort his disciples, he says, 'I say not that I will pray for you', that God may save you, I who yourselves shall see will die for you, I say not that I will pray for you, not I. But though I speak this to insinuate in the highest manner that I will, for if I spend my blood for you, will I not spend my breath for you? Yet the truth is, that the case so stands, that but for God's own ordination I should not need to do it, 'for the Father himself loves you'; that is, the Father of his own motion and proper good will, taken up of himself towards you, and not wrought in him by me, doth love you, and bears so much love to you, as he can deny you nothing, for he is 'your Father' as well as mine. How much more then shall you be saved when I shall strike in too, and use all my interest in him for you? Christ on purpose useth this speech, so to dash out of their hearts that conceit which harboureth in many of ours, who look upon God in the matter of salvation as one who is hardly entreated to come off to save sinners, and with whom Christ, through the backwardness of his heart, hath so much ado; and we are apt to think that when he doth come off to pardon, he doth it only and merely at Christ's entreaty, and for his sake, having otherwise no innate motion in himself sufficient to incline his heart to it; but that it is in this transaction by Christ with him, as a favourite procures a pardon for a traitor, whose person the king cares not for; only at his favourite's suit and request he grants it, which else he would never have done. You are deceived, says Christ, it is otherwise; my Father's heart is as much towards you, and for your salvation, as mine is; himself, of himself, loveth you. And the truth is, that God took up as vast a love unto us of himself at first as ever he hath borne us since, and all that Christ doth for us is but the expression of that love which was taken up originally in God's own heart. Thus we find that out of that love he gave Christ for us. So John 3:16, 'God so loved the world (of elect), that he gave his only begotten Son to die', *etc.* Yea, Christ's death was but a means to commend or set forth that love of his unto us. So Rom. 5:8. It was

God also that did himself give the persons unto Christ, and underhand set him on work to mediate for them. 'God was in Christ reconciling the world to himself': he only used Christ as his instrument to bring it honourably about. All the blessings he means to give us he first purposed and intended in himself (so Eph. 1:3, 5, 9, 11, compared) 'out of the good pleasure of his will', yet in Christ (as it is added there) as the means through which he would convey them; yea, Christ adds not one drop of love to God's heart, only draws it out; he broacheth it, and makes it flow forth, whose current had otherwise been stopped. The truth is, that God suborned Christ to beg them on our behalf for an honourable way of carrying it, as also to make us prize this favour the more; so as his heart is as ready to give all to us, as Christ's is to ask, and this out of his pure love to us.

The intercession therefore of Christ must needs speed, when God's heart is thus of itself prepared to us. In Isa. 53:10 it is said, 'The pleasure of the Lord shall prosper in his hand.' If our salvation be in Christ's hand, it is in a good hand; but if it be the pleasure of the Lord too, it must needs prosper. It is said of our hearts and prayers, that 'he prepareth the heart, and heareth the prayer';[1] much more therefore,

---

[1] A quotation from Goodwin's treatise *The Return of Prayers*,

when his own heart is prepared to grant the suit, will he easily hear it. When one hath a mind to do a thing, then the least hint procures it of him. So a father having a mind to spare his child, he will take any excuse, any one's mediation, even of a servant, a stranger, or an enemy, rather than of none. Now, when Christ shall speak for us, and speak God's own heart, how prevalent must those words need be! David's soul, 'longing to go forth unto Absalom', 2 Sam. 13:39, whom notwithstanding, for the honour of a father and a king's state policy, and to satisfy the world, he had banished the court for his treason; when Joab perceived it, that 'the king's heart was towards Absalom', chap. 14:1, and that the king only needed one to speak a good word for him, he suborns a woman, a stranger (no matter whom, for it had been all one for speeding), with a made tale to come to the king; and you know how easily it took and prevailed with him, and how glad the king's heart was of that occasion; even so acceptable it was to him, that Joab could not have done him a greater kindness, and that Joab knew well enough. Thus it is with God's heart towards us, Christ assures us of it, and you may believe him in this case. For Christ

---

which enjoyed great popularity and was published six years prior to *Christ Set Forth*. See Goodwin, *Works*, vol. 3, p. 387.—P.

might have took all the honour to himself, and made us beholden to himself alone for all God's kindness to us; but he deals plainly, and tells us that his Father is as ready as himself; and this he doth for his Father's honour and our comfort. And therefore it is that, John 17, in that this prayer so often cited in this discourse, he pleads our election, 'Thine they were, and thou gavest them me', verse 6. Thou commendedst them unto me, and badest me pray for them, and I do but commend the same to thee again. In the high priest's breastplate, when he went into the holy of holies, were set twelve stones, on which were written the names of the twelve tribes: the mystery of which is this, Christ bears us and our names in his heart when he goes to God; and moreover, we are God's jewels, precious in his own account and choice. So God calls them, Mal. 3:17; 'Made precious to him out of his love', so Isa. 43:4. So that God loves us as jewels chosen by him, but much more when he beholds us set and presented unto him in the breastplate of Christ's heart and prayer.

To conclude, therefore; we have now made both ends of this text to meet, God's love and Christ's intercession. The apostle began with that, 'Who shall accuse? It is God that justifies'; and he being for us, 'who can be against us?' The Father himself loves us, as he is our Father. And then he ends with this, 'Christ intercedes', namely, with our Father and his Father, 'who then shall condemn?' Who or what can possibly condemn, all these things being for us, the least of which were alone enough to save us?

Let us now look round about, and take a full view and prospect at once, of all those particulars that Christ hath done and doth for us, and their several and joint influence which they have into our salvation.

1. In that Christ died, it assures us of a perfect price paid for, and a right to eternal life thereby acquired.

2. In that he rose again as a common person, this assures us yet further that there is a formal, legal, and irrevocable act of justification of us passed and enrolled in that court of heaven between Christ and God; and that in his being then justified, we were also justified in him, so that thereby our justification is made past recalling.

3. Christ's ascension into heaven is a further act of his taking possession of heaven for us, he then formally entering upon that our right in our stead; and so is a further confirmation of our salvation to us. But still we in our own persons are not yet saved, this being but done to us as we are representatively in Christ as our head.

4. Therefore he sits at God's right hand, which

imports his being armed and invested with 'all power in heaven and earth, to give and apply eternal life to us'.

5. And last of all there remains intercession, to finish and complete our salvation; to do the thing, even to save us. And as Christ's death and resurrection were to procure our *justification*, so his sitting at God's right hand and intercession are to procure *salvation*; and by faith we may see it done, and behold our souls not only sitting in heaven, as in Christ a common person sitting there in our right, as an evidence that we shall come thither; but also through Christ's intercession begun, we may see ourselves actually possessed of heaven. And there I will leave all you that are believers by faith possessed of it, and solacing your souls in it, and do you fear condemnation if you can.

Chapter 10

The use of all; containing some encouragements for weak believers, from Christ's intercession, out of Heb. 7:25.

Now, for a conclusion of this discourse, I will add a brief use of encouragement; and this, suited to the lowest faith of the weakest believer, who cannot put forth any act of assurance, and is likewise discouraged from coming in unto Christ. And I shall confine myself only unto what those most comfortable words, as any in the book of God, do hold forth, which the apostle hath uttered concerning Christ's intercession, the point in hand: 'Wherefore he is able to save to the utmost those that come to God by him, seeing he ever liveth to make intercession for them',—words which I have had the most recourse unto in this doctrinal part of any other, as most tending to the clearing of many things about intercession; and which I would also commend to and leave with poor believers, to have recourse unto for their comfort, as a sufficient abundary[1] of consolation unto their souls, and as a *catholicon* or universal cordial against all faintings and misgivings of spirit whatsoever.

In the words observe,

1. A definition of faith by the lowest acts of it, for the comfort of weak Christians.

2. Encouragements unto such a faith, opposite to all misgivings and discouragements whatsoever.

1. A definition of faith; and such as will suit the weakest believers. It is a coming unto God by Christ for salvation.

---

[1] overflowing, abundant source. — P.

(1.) It is *a coming* to be saved. Let not the want of assurance that God will save thee, or that Christ is thine, discourage thee, if thou hast but a heart to come to God by Christ to be saved, though thou knowest not whether he will yet save thee or no. Remember that the believers of the New Testament are here described to be comers to God by Christ; such as go out of themselves, and rest in nothing in themselves, do come unto God through Christ for salvation, though with trembling.

(2.) It is a coming unto God. For he is the ultimate object of our faith, and the person with whom we have to do in believing, and from whom we are to receive salvation, if ever we obtain it.

(3.) It is a coming unto God *by Christ*; which phrase is used in this epistle, in an allusion to the worshippers of the Old Testament, who, when they had sinned, were directed to go to God by a priest, who with a sacrifice made an atonement for them. Now Christ is the great and true high priest, 'by whom we have access to the Father', Eph. 2:18. The word is προσαγωγὴν [*prosagogen*], a leading by the hand. Dost thou not know how to appear before God, or to come to him? Come first to Christ, and he will take thee by the hand, and go along with thee, and lead thee to his Father.

(4.) It is a coming unto God by Christ *for salvation*. Many a poor soul is apt to think that in coming to God by faith, it must not aim at itself, or its own salvation. Yes, it may: for that is here made the errand or business which faith hath with God in coming to him, or which it comes for; and this is secretly couched in these words, for the apostle, speaking of the very aim of the heart in coming, he therefore on purpose mentions Christ's ability to save: 'he is able *to save*'.

2. Secondly, here are many encouragements to such a faith as is not yet grown up unto assurance of salvation.

(1.) Here is the most suitable object propounded unto it, namely, Christ as interceding; which work of intercession, because it remains for Christ as yet to do for a soul that is to be saved, and which he is every day a-doing for us; therefore it is more peculiarly fitted unto a recumbent faith. For, when such a soul comes and casts itself upon Christ, that thing in Christ which must needs most suit that kind of act is that which is yet to be done by Christ for that soul. Now for that soul to come to Christ to die for it, and offer up himself a sacrifice (as sinners did use to come to the high priest to sacrifice for them), this were bootless, for (as it is, verse 27) he hath at 'once done that' already. And as for what is already past and done, such a believer's faith is oftentimes exceedingly puzzled what manner of act to put forth towards Christ about; as (for example) when it is about to come unto God, and it hears of an election of some unto salvation from all eternity made by him; because this is an act already passed by God, the soul knows it to be in vain to cast itself upon God for election or to come unto him to elect and choose itself. And so, in like manner, when the soul looks upon Christ's death, because it is done and past, it knows not how to take it in believing, when it wanteth assurance that Christ died for it, though it should come to Christ to be saved by virtue of his death. But there is this one work that remains still to be done by him for us, and which he is daily a-doing, and that is, interceding; for he lives ever to intercede or to pray for us, in the strength and merit of that his sacrifice once offered up. This therefore is more directly and peculiarly fitted unto a faith of recumbency, or of coming unto Christ; the proper act of such a faith (as it is distinguished from faith of assurance) being a casting one's self upon Christ for something it would have done or wrought for one. Hence intercession becomes a fit object for the aim and errand of such a faith in this its coming to Christ, as also 'to be saved' is; it being a thing yet to be wrought and accomplished for me by Christ, is therefore a fit mark for such a faith to level at in its coming to Christ. Those acts of God and Christ which are past, faith of assurance doth more easily comply with: such a faith takes in with comfort that Christ hath died for me, and risen again, and doth now intercede for me, and so I shall certainly be saved; but so cannot this weak faith do. Come thou therefore unto Christ, as to save thee through his death past, and by the merit of it, so for the present, and for the time to come, to take thy cause in hand, and to intercede for thee: it is a great relief unto such a faith (as cannot put forth acts of assurance, that what hath been done by Christ hath been done for it), that God hath left Christ this work yet to do for us. So as the intercession of Christ may afford matter to such a faith to throw itself upon Christ, to perform it for us, and it may set a-work to do it.

(2.) Now if such a soul ask, But will Christ, upon my coming to him for salvation, be set a-work to intercede for me, and undertake my cause?

I answer it out of those words, 'He lives to intercede for them who come to God by him.' He lives on purpose to perform this work; it is the end of his living, the business of his life. And as he received a commandment to die, and it was the end of his life on earth, so he hath received a command to intercede, and to be a common high priest for all that come to God by him. God hath appointed him to this work by an oath, 'He sware, and would not repent, Thou shalt be a priest for ever, after the order of Melchisedec': and this is the end of his life in heaven. That as in the old law the high priest (Christ's type in this) 'ought to offer up the sacrifice' of every one that came unto God by him (as Heb. 5:5), in like manner Christ; for it is his calling, as you have it, verse 6. Otherwise, as that woman said to Philip, when she came to him for justice, and he put her off, Then cease (says she) to be a king: so if Christ should deny any such soul to take its cause in hand, he must then cease to be a priest. He lives to intercede; he is a priest called by God, as was Aaron, verse 6. Wherefore he ought to do it, in that it is his office.

(3.) And if thy soul yet feareth the difficulty of its own particular case, in respect of the greatness of thy sins, and the circumstances thereof, or any consideration whatsoever, which to thy view doth make thy salvation an hard suit to obtain: the apostle therefore further adds, 'He is able to save to the utmost', whatever thy cause be, and this through this his intercession. That same word, 'to the utmost', is a good word, and well put in for our comfort. Consider it therefore, for it is a reaching word, and extends itself so far, that thou canst not look beyond it. Let thy soul be set upon the highest mount that ever any creature was yet set upon, and that is enlarged to take in and view the most spacious prospect both of sin and misery, and difficulties of being saved, that ever yet any poor humbled soul did cast within itself: yea, join to these all the objections and hindrances of thy salvation that the heart of man can suppose or invent against itself: lift up thy eyes and look to the utmost thou canst see, and Christ by his intercession is able to save thee beyond the horizon and furthest compass of thy thoughts, even 'to the utmost' and worst case the heart of man can suppose. It is not thy having lain long in sin, long under terrors and despairs, or having sinned often after many enlightenings, that can hinder thee from being saved by Christ. Do but remember this same word, 'to the utmost', and then put in what exceptions thou wilt or canst, lay all the bars in thy way that are imaginable; yet know thou that 'the gates of hell shall not prevail against thee'.

(4.) Again, consider but what it is that Christ, who hath by his death done enough to save thee, doth yet further for thee in heaven. If thou thoughtest thou hadst all the saints in heaven and earth jointly concurring in promoving[1] thy salvation, and competitors unto God in instant and incessant requests and prayers to save thee, how wouldst thou be encouraged? Shall I tell thee? One word out of Christ's mouth (who is the King of saints) will do more than all in heaven and earth can do: and what is there then which we may not hope to obtain through his intercession?

And wouldst thou know whether he hath undertaken thy cause, and begun to intercede for thee? In a word, Hath he put his Spirit into thy heart, and set thy own heart on work to make incessant intercessions for thyself 'with groans unutterable' (as the apostle hath it, Rom. 8)? This is the echo of Christ's intercession for thee in heaven.

(5.) And lastly; if such a soul shall further object, But will he not give over suing for me? May I not be cast out of his prayers through my unbelief? Let it here be considered that he lives 'ever' to intercede: and therefore, if he once undertake thy cause, and getteth thee into his prayers, he will never leave thee out, night nor day. He intercedeth ever, till he hath accomplished and finished thy salvation. Men have been cast out of good and holy men's prayers, as Saul out of Samuel's, and the people of Israel out

---

[1] moving forward, promoting. — P.

of Jeremiah's, but never out of Christ's prayers; the 'smoke of his incense ascends for ever', and he will intercede to the utmost, till he hath saved thee to the utmost. He will never give over, but will lie in the dust for thee, or he will perfect and procure thy salvation.

Only, whilst I am thus raising up your faith to him upon the work of his intercession for us, let me speak a word to you for him, so to stir up your love to him, upon the consideration of this his intercession also. You see you have the whole life of Christ, first and last, both here and in heaven, laid out for you. He had not come to earth but for you, he had no other business here. 'Unto us a Son is born.' And, to be sure, he had not died but for you. 'For us a Son was given'; and when he rose, it was 'for your justification'. And now he is gone to heaven, he lives but to intercede for you. He makes your salvation his constant calling. O therefore, let us live wholly unto him, for he hath and doth live wholly unto us. You have his whole time among you; and if he were your servant, you could desire no more. There was much of your time lost before you began to live to him; but there hath been no moment of his time which he hath not lived to, and improved for you. Nor are you able ever to live for him but only in this life, for hereafter you shall live with him, and be glorified of him. I conclude all with that of the apostle, 'The love of Christ it should constrain us', because we cannot but 'judge' this to be the most equal, that 'they which live should not henceforth live unto themselves, but unto him who died for them, and rose again', and (out of the text I also add) 'sits at God's right hand'; yea, and there 'lives for ever to make intercession for us'.